TRUING-UP

OF

AEROPLANES.

Air Department,
    1st September 1916.
      No. 5.

The Naval & Military Press Ltd

Published by

The Naval & Military Press Ltd
Unit 5 Riverside, Brambleside,
Bellbrook Industrial Estate,
Uckfield, East Sussex,
TN22 1QQ England

Tel: +44 (0) 1825 749494
Fax: +44 (0) 1825 765701

www.naval-military-press.com
www.nmarchive.com

The Library & Archives Department at the Royal Armouries Museum, Leeds, specialises in the history and development of armour and weapons from earliest times to the present day. Material relating to the development of artillery and modern fortifications is held at the Royal Armouries Museum, Fort Nelson.

For further information contact:
Royal Armouries Museum, Library, Armouries Drive, Leeds, West Yorkshire LS10 1LT
Royal Armouries, Library, Fort Nelson, Down End Road, Fareham PO17 6AN

Or visit the Museum's website at
www.armouries.org.uk

In reprinting in facsimile from the original, any imperfections are inevitably reproduced and the quality may fall short of modern type and cartographic standards.

CHAPTER I.

General Principles.

A.—Selection of Materials.

Before commencing to erect an aeroplane care must be exercised in the examination of all parts to be used. Attention must be paid to the following:—

(1) *Metal Parts.*—There must be no signs of rust or flaws, especially in the wires.

(2) Bolts and nuts employed should be accurately machined all over.

(3) Piano or spoke wire should not have been previously bent and must be free from kinks.

(4) Stranded wire or cable should be regularly twisted and not frayed at any point.

There should be no trace of white powdery deposit on the lay of wire rope. All splices should have at least two complete tucks before the strands are tapered, and the splices should be served with waxed cord or wire.

Extra flexible cable is to be invariably employed for all controls. In other parts of the machine where cable is employed flexible cable of 7×7 or 1×19 construction is to be employed. These latter types of cable do not splice so well as the extra flexible, but a more efficient joint than that obtained by splicing may be made in the following manner:—

The end of the wire cable is bent round to form an eye, and the parts of the cable which are thus brought into contact are carefully tinned, and then either served round with a series of bands of copper wire or fitted with a series of flattened copper ferrules. If wire serving is employed the serving must not be too neatly done, but the wire is to be wound round the two parts of the cable so as to leave small spaces of about twice the diameter of the wire between adjacent coils. In addition, about $\frac{3}{8}$-inch of bare cable should be left between adjacent ferrules or bands of wire serving. These latter, and also the bare cable between them, are then carefully soldered over. When soldering or tinning, a blow lamp is on no account to be used. An ordinary soldering iron is to be employed.

This type of joint should never give an efficiency of less than 100 per cent. The thimble employed in the eye should be of solid construction, and the hole through which the eye of the cable passes should have a suitable radius as in the case of spliced wire.

(5) Tubing should be perfectly straight and should not show signs of having been previously bent and subsequently

straightened. The inside should be carefully inspected for signs of rust; it should then be carefully oiled internally and its ends should be finally plugged with wood to prevent the entrance of water or damp.

(6) The threads of bolts, nuts and screws should be clean, and not worn or burred, and there should be no slackness in the nut.

(7) Strut sockets and other metal fittings should not be bent out of their original shape. Such fittings should also not be used if they show signs of having been bent and subsequently straightened. In the case of aluminium sockets, care must be taken that there are no cracks, especially where the sockets have been previously subjected to severe stress. Eye-plates and eye-bolts should show no signs of wear or fracture.

(8) Metal work must either be bent hot all over or bent cold; local heating must not be employed unless carried out along the whole width of the plate.

(9) Sticky tape should never be used to cover up strainers or ferrules, or to bind wires where they cross. The tape does not provide protection against rust and it hides the rust when formed. When employed on strainers it also prevents the locking-wire from being seen. Where bracing wires cross they should not, as a general rule, be bound together unless they touch and so are liable to chafe one against the other. In this case it is necessary to bind the wires, when waxed twine or iron wire only is to be employed.

(10) Great care should be taken that all bracing wire is fully stretched before being used, or the machine will soon go "soggy" and need re-truing. This stretching can best be done by putting a proof load on to the finished wire, after splicing (if possible) equal to the normal load which will be borne by it in flight. Heavy gauge thimbles should be employed in the eye of a splice so as to prevent the eye elongating, and the attachment holding the eye should have a sufficient radius to prevent it from closing the top of the eye.

Wood Parts.—The correct wood for the various parts of the aeroplanes must always be employed. There should be no signs of flaws and the wood should be properly seasoned. Struts must be straight; any departure from a straight line is liable to be accentuated by end pressure to a sufficient extent to involve collapse or fracture. Signs of dry rot and wormholes should be looked for most carefully before varnishing.

Fabric.—Fabric should show no signs of deterioration. In covering a plane, fabric that has already been doped should not be re-employed.

B.—*Fitting of Accessory Parts.*

(1) All internal drift wirings and any metallic fixings covered by the fabric must be painted with some rust- and dope-resisting material, such as "Velure" enamel or "Velure"

varnish. If enamel is employed it should be of light colour, otherwise it may hide rust when the latter has once formed.

(2) *Turnbuckles or Wire Strainers.*—
- (a) Turnbuckles should be a good fit on the screwed ends of the barrel. There should be no "shake" between the two parts nor should they be too tight a fit. The thread should be perfectly uniform. In the event of the turnbuckle being a tight fit, there is a risk of the wires being twisted in tightening up.
- (b) Turnbuckles must not be worked upon with pliers or other tools. A wire, passed through the hole provided in the barrel, must be employed when adjusting them, the eyebolts being held by the fingers or a wire.
- (c) Turnbuckles must not be screwed up to the limit of their screw threads. The wire itself must be shortened when necessary, or a new one fitted.
- (d) Turnbuckles must always have the whole of their thread engaged, and the barrel must not be covered with tape.
- (e) *In no circumstances is it permissible to saw off any portion of the turnbuckle.*

(3) *Lubrication of Pulleys, &c.*—All pulleys and fair leads for the wires must be lubricated with grease and not with oil.

(4) *Fitting of cocks.*—In all cases where cocks are employed in petrol or oil systems, care is to be taken that they are so fitted that when in their correct working positions their handles point downwards, otherwise the effect of vibration will tend to alter their setting. In cases where cocks have T handles, arrangements must be made to secure them in their working positions.

(5) *Petrol and Oil Piping.*—Piping of all kinds must be arranged with a proper regard to the amount of vibration to which it will be subjected. Long unsupported lengths must be avoided. In metal piping it is generally advisable to insert a joint of specially prepared rubber tubing close to any unions, as the latter frequently become a seat of fracture. Although the special rubber tubing is prepared to resist the action of petrol and oil, it will nevertheless gradually deteriorate, and will require examination at short intervals, though this can be partially avoided by keeping the ends of the copper tubes close together. Chokes in pipes are frequently caused by deterioration of the lining of the tubing.

(6) *Bolts and Nuts.*—Care must be taken that when small bolts and nuts are tightened up with a spanner they are not overstrained.

If a nut be tightened up too much the bolt will have an initial stress put into it, and the further stress due to its normal load may be sufficient to cause the bolt to fracture. Where bolts are fitted on wooden members of an aeroplane, washers of ample diameter are to be fitted under the head of the bolt and the nut to prevent these from crushing the wood when tightened up.

(7) *Locking Devices.*—All bolts and nuts, &c., must be secured in some *positive manner* to prevent them from slacking back. An ordinary split pin fitted above a nut is useless for the purpose, unless the nut is washered up to the split pin and the nut a tight fit on the bolt.

The following are the most general methods of securing nuts:—

(a) Castellated nut fitted with split pin.
(b) End of bolt (or stud) riveted over the top of the nut.
(c) Check nut fitted over an ordinary nut, and a split pin fitted to bear on the upper nut.
(d) The thread at the end of the bolt may only be burred in exceptional cases, such as when fitted in an inaccessible place.
(e) Spring washers are often fitted underneath nuts, but this is *not* a positive lock.
(f) With turnbuckles, a wire is fitted passing through the hole in the barrel and secured to both eyebolts. Great care must be taken that the keep wire is put on properly.
(g) Before putting fabric on to the wings or other parts the greatest care should be taken that all nuts are locked in the requisite manner, that all turnbuckles are fitted with keep wires, and that all internal steel work is protected by a good quality paint or varnish against the formation of rust.

(8) *Tension of Bracing Wires.*—Wires which are in inaccessible places, such as the internal wiring of wings, are usually put on with rather greater initial tension than ones which can be easily tested.

(9) *Notes on Covering and Doping of Planes.*—It is found that the best dopes at present on the market are those made by Messrs. Cellon and Messrs. The British Emaillite Company. Both these firms manufacture non-poisonous dopes which for every reason are preferable to those containing tetrachlorethane.

"Emaillite" 11a and c, or "Cellon" N.P. 2 are dopes to be recommended.

Both of the firms mentioned above now issue comprehensive "Doping Schemes," the instructions contained in which must be rigidly adhered to in order to obtain satisfactory results. In the case of machines to be used in tropical climates "Cellon" should be used, and the upper surfaces of the wings finally varnished with an approved non-actinic pigment varnish, such as P.C. 10, a khaki-coloured acetate paint, which protects the dope from the actinic rays of the sun's light, thereby preventing decomposition.

The under surfaces of the wings should receive two coats of some approved transparent varnish, such as V. 114.

When covering planes prior to doping, the surfaces of the wing-framework in contact with the fabric should be left bare and not varnished.

The fabric is to be put on in the approved manner either by—
  (1) Sewing to the ribs, or
  (2) Fixing it down by cane strips.

If the first method is employed, the string is to be waxed to prevent its becoming slack. It must be further secured by a double knot at three points along the length of the rib, so that in case of the string breaking the whole of the fabric does not become loose on the rib; the pitch of the stitch must not exceed 4 inches, except in the case of abnormally large machines.

If method 2 is employed, brass screws must be used to secure the cane strips, which must be carefully bored to avoid splitting.

The joints in the fabric should be made of the balloon seam type with double stitching, and the fabric should be laid over the leading edge and sewn up to the trailing edge. The fabric should be fairly taut, but *not too* taut, before doping is commenced.

When doping with "Cellon" or "Emaillite," the first coat should be put on with about 2 parts dope, 1 part thinning; the second coat 4 parts dope, 1 part thinning, then three or more coats of undiluted dope.

The surface of the wing should be finished up with 2 coats of Pigment Varnish. The fabric must on no account be sand-papered to obtain a smooth surface. Pigment Varnish is employed on the upper surfaces of wings, &c., only, and its object is to form a screen through which the actinic rays of light from the sun cannot pass, and thus to protect the fabric from deterioration under the action of sunlight.

Doping should be carried out in as dry an atmosphere as possible. Successive coats of dope are to be put on as soon as the preceding coat is dry.

(10) *Fabric on Fuselage.*—In machines whose fuselage is covered with fabric, it is the Admiralty practice to have the joint in the fabric laced so as to provide a ready means of inspecting the fuselage or tuning it up.

If the lacing is carried out with a single cord, then in the event of the cord breaking, the cover of the fuselage is liable to strip off, foul the elevator and prevent it from working. When lacing up fuselages, the cord is to be securely fastened *by double knots* at *every 12th pair of eyes*, so as to prevent the cover from stripping off in the event of the lace breaking.

CHAPTER II.

Tractor Biplanes.

The first operation to be proceeded with is the truing-up of the fuselage.

Truing-up of the Fuselage. — The usual method of construction adopted in the fuselage is that indicated in the diagram (Figs. 1 a and b).

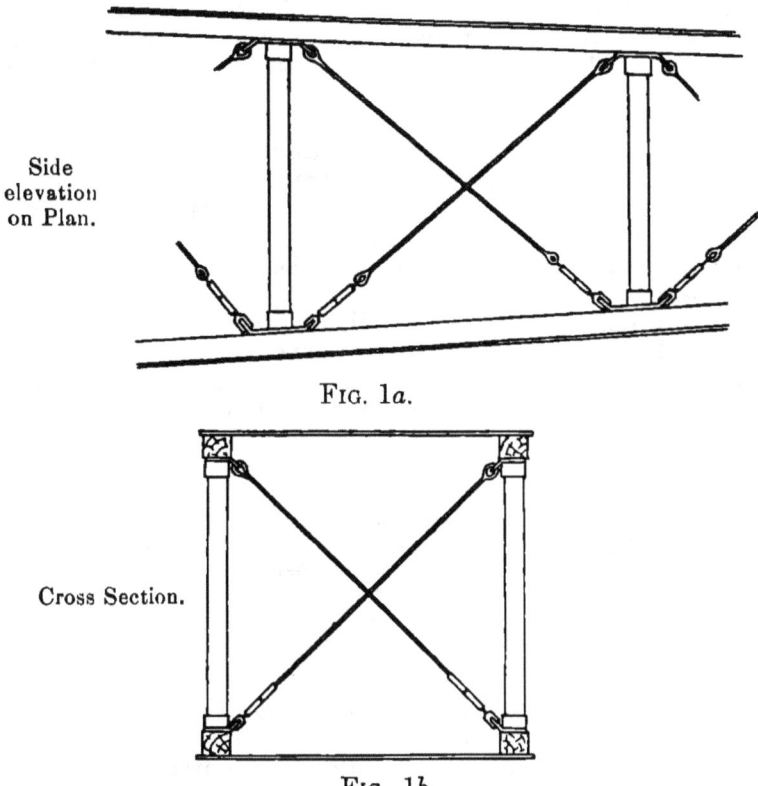

Side elevation on Plan.

Fig. 1a.

Cross Section.

Fig. 1b.

The fuselage is a braced structure, usually of rectangular section. The four longitudinal members or "longerons" are connected at intervals by vertical and horizontal struts which form transverse frames or panels of more or less rectangular or trapezoidal shape. Each of the panels formed by the longerons and a pair of these struts are braced together with diagonal wiring, so as to make each panel into a stiff frame and so render the fuselage structure capable of taking the bending moment due to the tail loading, rudder, &c.

The transverse sections are similarly traced by diagonal wires which run transversely across the inside of the fuselage forming the panels, having the main longerons for corners. These provide the fuselage with the necessary rigidity to resist torsion.

The bracing wires are usually fitted with turnbuckles which enable their lengths to be adjusted within limits, and so allow of the fuselage being trued up. In B.E. machines swaged rods are fitted in place of the bracing wires. The butted ends of these are threaded opposite hands and screw into fork-end attachments which render them adjustable.

In most of the machines built by Messrs. Short the bracing wires are made dead to length, and no provision is made for adjusting them when truing up, other than a small amount of play in the "U" bolts which form their attachment to the fuselage longerons.

It is of great importance that the head resistance of the fuselage should be as small as possible. The longitudinal members are, therefore, curved to give it as nearly as possible a streamline form. At the same time the fuselage must be a rigid structure, otherwise it will whip when the controls are worked and so bring excessive stresses to bear on its component members.

The majority of fuselages built at present date are of one of two distinct types; in the first type the upper and lower longerons are curved symmetrically both in the horizontal and vertical planes about the axis of the fuselage, e.g., the B.E. biplane (see Fig. 2).

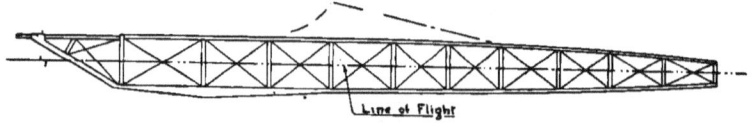

Fig. 2.

In the other type, of which the Sopwith machine is an example, the top longerons are straight except for the short portion at the nose while the lower ones are curved (see Fig. 3).

In machines of the former type the line of flight is parallel to the axis of the fuselage, while in the latter it is parallel to the upper longeron in the normal flying position. In practically all machines the datum line from which the machine is tuned up, whether parallel to the axis or to the upper longeron, is parallel to the centre line of the crankshaft. As will be seen later, this gives a line from which all pusher machines can be trued up. It is obvious that if any of the bracing wires become altered in length the whole of the structure may alter in shape and so get out of truth, and since its length is great compared with the cross section, any such alteration will have an exaggerated effect on the trim of the machine. It is therefore necessary that the fuselage should be periodically checked for true alignment, and, if necessary, re-trued up. The foremost consideration in connection with a fuselage is that its axis shall be true.

Symmetrical Type Fuselage.—With this type of fuselage, when under construction, each of the transverse struts, on all four sides of the fuselage, is bisected in length and the middle point marked as at (a) (Fig. 4).

It is the Admiralty practice that all contractors shall permanently mark in these points with black paint.

If the fuselage structure is in truth, a line stretched between two points at the middle of the struts situated at each of its ends will cut each of the intermediate struts at its middle point. If they do not, the fuselage is out of truth, and the diagonal bracing wires must be suitably readjusted until these points come truly in line.

If the fuselage is very much out of truth, the operation of truing up is much facilitated by the following procedure:—

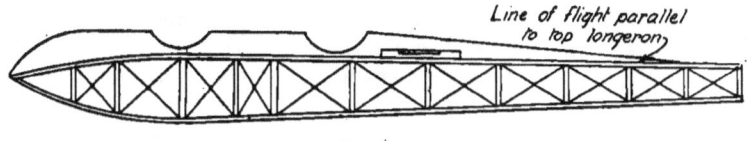

Fig. 3.

The intersection of the centre lines of each of the strut ends and of the longitudinal members is accurately marked with a dot, as shown in Fig. 4. If the panel BCDE is in truth the points A and A^1 will both be situated on the axis of the side of the fuselage, and in this case it is obvious from the symmetrical form of the fuselage that the two diagonals of the panel, viz., BD and CE, will be equal. On the other hand, if A^1 is not on the axis of the side of the fuselage, then one of these diagonals will be greater than the other.

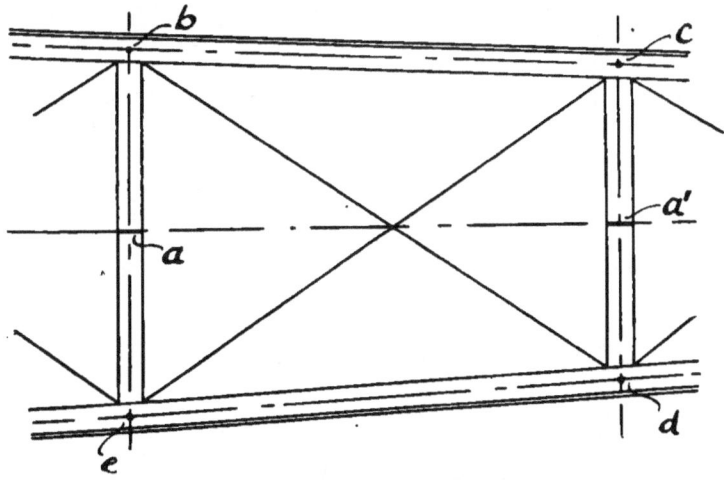

Fig. 4.

This method of truing up a fuselage of this type is carried out as follows:—The fuselage is placed on trestles and, commencing with one of the side panels at its forward end, the distance between the diagonal points B and D is measured with a trammel and checked against the length of the other diagonal CE. Should these diagonals be unequal, then by slackening out one diagonal wire and tightening up the other, the panel can be adjusted until they are equal.

The operation is then repeated on the next panel, and so on along the whole fuselage.

When truing up by this method, great care must be taken to see that all the strut sockets are fitted to the longerons in their exact and true positions. If one socket is out of place, it will cause the diagonals of each of the panels on either side of it to be of uneven length.

If the fuselage is being completely built up, this can be checked by putting the longerons alongside each other, and comparing the positions for the struts as marked on the longerons. If, however, the fuselage is already built up and only requires re-truing, the position of the strut sockets can be checked by a plumb bob on set square or spirit level.

As a check on the foregoing method of truing up, and also in cases where the fuselage is only slightly out of truth, the alignment of the fuselage should be checked by a line stretched along the length of the fuselage coinciding with the middle points of the struts at each of its ends. This line can be tied directly on to the forward strut, but at the aft end, owing to the taper of the fuselage, it will be necessary to clamp a batten across one of the after frames, and to attach the line to this well clear of the fuselage so as to leave the line free to take up its true position. The line must be kept very taut during the process of truing up and not allowed to sag at all. The coincidence of the line and the points marked at the middle of the intermediate struts can be checked approximately by eye, but as a final check it should be tested at several points by squaring off from the side of the struts to the string with a square (see Fig. 5), or, in the case of tapered strut-members, by means of a level.

If the middle point on the length of any strut is off the centre line of the fuselage, it should be brought to its correct position by slackening off the bracing wires which come to one end of the strut and tightening the opposing wires at its other end. As has already been stated, it is most convenient to start work at the forward end of the fuselage and get this true, and then to work gradually to the aft end. Since errors may occur in joining the strut socket positions on the longerons, the alignment of the centre line of the fuselage is to be the final check for the trueness of the fuselage structure.

Having got the sides of the fuselage into true alignment a similar procedure is adopted to true up or check its top and bottom surfaces.

The panels of these surfaces are cross-wired in the usual manner, but in addition the four longerons are braced together so as to give the fuselage torsional rigidity. Consequently, if any panel of either the upper or lower surface of the fuselage is found not in truth, then, before any adjustments of the panel wiring are made, care must be taken to see that these bracing wires which are in a plane perpendicular to the axis of the fuselage are sufficiently slack to allow the requisite adjustment to be made in the upper and lower horizontal panels without causing them to be overbraced.

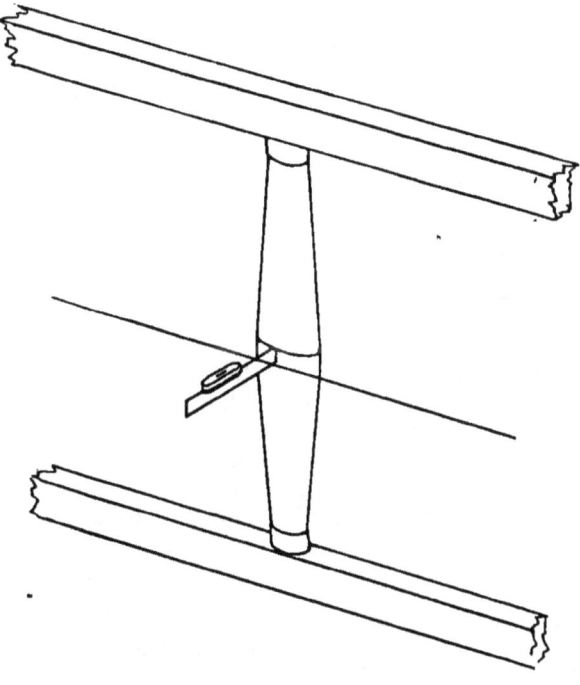

Fig. 5.

In the case of B.E. machines the upper and lower surfaces of the fuselage are filled in with three-ply wood. These panels should therefore remain permanently in truth; should they, however, get damaged and out of truth, they can only be adjusted by fitting new three-ply. In such a case it is probable that new longerons would also be required.

The next operation consists of "squaring up" the fuselage by means of the transverse bracing wires already referred to. These transverse wires bring the sides and upper surface of the fuselage perpendicular to each other. The operation of truing up may be considerably facilitated by employing a sliding trammel. This instrument consists of two light battens held together by metal clips which allow the two battens to slide over but keep them parallel to each other, so that their total length can be easily adjusted. The length of a diagonal of any one panel can thus be measured and compared with that of the opposite diagonal of the same panel (*see* Fig. 6). Should the two diagonals of any one transverse panel not be equal, the diagonal bracing wires are adjusted until they are so, and the sides of the fuselage are then of necessity perpendicular to one another.

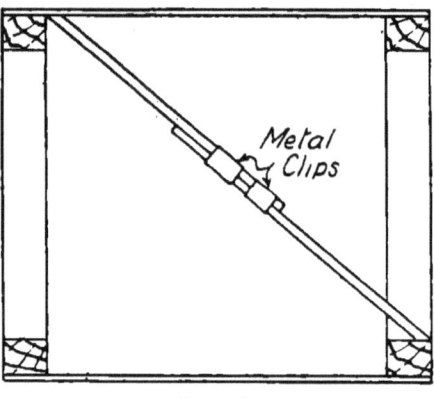

FIG. 6.

When the transverse panels at the front of the fuselage have been checked and found true, the adjustment of the remainder of the cross wires can also be fairly accurately checked by sighting along the length of the fuselage from the forward cross wires to the middle of the stern post; all the remaining cross wires should intersect along this line of sight, which, if the fuselage is true, will be the centre line of the whole fuselage structure.

Fuselages of the "Sopwith" type.—With this type of structure the procedure of checking the alignment or setting-up is rendered more simple than in the former case by the top longerons being absolutely straight for their whole length. It is only necessary to check this straightness of the longerons to ensure that the side panelling of the fuselage is true. This can be very simply carried out by employing a long straight-edge placed in contact with the top of these longerons and then adjusting the diagonal bracing wires of the panels till straightness is secured. For ordinary checking purposes, if no straight-edge is available, a string should be stretched taut along the top of each upper longeron, level with its upper surface. If this string is kept to one side of the longeron's surface, so as to be free to take up a straight position, it will provide a good guide as to the alignment. When the sides have been lined up correctly, the truing up of the panels of the top and bottom surfaces of the fuselage and the "squaring up" of its cross section panels may be proceeded with in exactly the same manner as has already been described for the former type of body structure.

Initial tension of Bracing Wires.—The greatest care must be taken in adjusting the tension of all bracing wires, otherwise they may be set up sufficiently overstrained to cause them either to break themselves or to deform the structure when the additional flying load is put upon them. In all cases a panel must be adjusted by first slacking off one diagonal and then tightening the other.

When the adjustments are completed and the machine is correctly trued up, the bracing wires *should all be taut*, and care should be taken to ensure that *the degree of tension is uniform throughout the whole of the various panels* of the fuselage. This presents no great difficulty so far as the panels of the outer surface of the fuselage are concerned, but in certain cases may prove difficult as regards the transverse bracing.

If the initial tension in any wire is excessive, not only is the wire likely to fail when additional forces are brought to bear on it in flight, but large compressive stresses are thrown on to the compression members, even if the wire does not actually fail. Further, if the initial tension of the bracing wires varies in different panels, some of the members may commence to give and so throw the whole structure of the fuselage out of truth the first time the machine is taken into the air.

In certain cases where a machine comes into the workshops to be trued up, it may be found that by merely slightly slacking off certain bracing wires true alignment may be regained.

When in the course of truing up a structure it is necessary to tighten up one or more wires and at the same time slack off others in the same or adjacent panels, the slacking off should invariably be carried out first.

The final operation in truing up with regard to the fuselage is to check the position of the main-wing spar sockets. These should be fixed absolutely symmetrically on each side of the fuselage, otherwise difficulties will be experienced when fitting the wings.

The vertical distances from the upper longerons to the centres of the main wing spar sockets should first be checked from the drawing; if no drawing is available it will suffice if these measurements are equal for the corresponding sockets on each side of the fuselage.

Next, the positions of these sockets must be symmetrical along the length of the fuselage; this can be checked in the following manner.

With the fuselage still fixed on trestles and with its axis level fore-and-aft and top surface level athwart-ship, run a plumb-line up from the centre of each main-wing spar socket on to the top of the upper longeron.

Where this line meets the upper surface of the longeron, mark, by means of a square, a pencil line across the upper surface of the longerons. The point of intersection of this line with the centre line of the longerons should then be marked by a dot or, still better, a pin. The distance of each of these points (each pair being taken separately) to the centre of the rudder post, or some other convenient point known to be in vertical plane through the centre line of the fuselage, is then taken with a steel tape. These should be equal for each pair of points. If these distances are not equal, then either the spar sockets are out of their symmetrical positions, or else the fuselage itself is out of truth.

* Truing up the Plane.—The next procedure is to true up the main planes. The usual form of construction employed in wings is shown diagrammatically in Fig. 7. The main framework comprises two main spars "aa" and "bb" and a certain number of main ribs "cc" fixed at right angles to these main spars. The rectangles or panels formed by the intersection of the main ribs or drift struts and the main spars are braced together by means of diagonal bracing wires which form the wing structure into a rigidly braced structure, and give the wing sufficient rigidity to resist the drift forces brought to bear on it during flight.

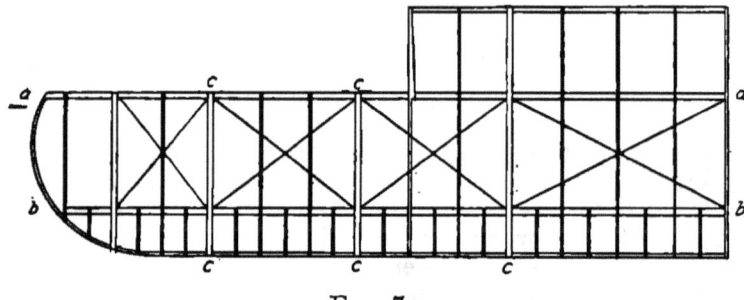

Fig. 7.

But for this bracing the wing would fold back under the action of these drift forces. A number of light ribs are fitted in between the main ribs in order to support the fabric in an efficient manner and give the whole wing section the necessary profile or section.

The most common type of wing structure is very simple to true up, since the front and rear spars of the main planes are rigidly parallel. To check this alignment the intersection of the centre lines of the spars and the main drift struts or compression ribs are accurately found and marked with a hard pencil. The trueness of the wing structure is then tested by taking each separate panel in turn and comparing the lengths of its diagonals by means of a trammel. If in any particular panel the lengths of the two diagonals are found to be unequal they

---

* It is of the utmost importance that when a plane has to be supported on trestles, the trestles shall be placed under the main spars, and not under the lighter ribs, which have very little strength, and so are likely to get deranged if carelessly handled.

must be made equal by adjusting the lengths of the diagonal bracing wires in the manner already described for truing up the fuselage. When each panel has been dealt with in this way the whole wing should be in perfect alignment.

When erecting a new plane or adjusting an old one, great care must be taken to see that the strut sockets or box rib fastenings are exactly opposite each other on their respective spars. This can be done by direct measurement or by placing the spars alongside each other before commencing erection of the wings. If the box ribs or drift struts are not fixed in their true positions on the main spars, the diagonals in each panel will not be equal, hence it is necessary to check their positions most carefully.

When all the panels have been trued up in this manner both front and rear spars should be perfectly straight along the whole of their respective lengths. This should be checked either by testing with a straight-edge or else by stretching a line along the spars, on top of each spar and just over its edge, and then observing whether the edge of the spar is parallel to the string along its whole length. The straightness of the spars must be taken as the final test for the true alignment of the wing structure.

In the case of the Henry Farman and similar types of wings, the spars of the main planes are not parallel to each other, and the wings must be trued up by getting the rear spar straight along its whole length and at the same time perpendicular to the end or box rib of the centre plane.

This is best carried out as follows:—

(1) Take the centre panel of the plane, and since the main spars are parallel in this panel, true the panel up by adjusting the diagonal bracing till the diagonals of the panel are equal.

(2) The next panel outboard on either side of the centre panel can be trued up in a similar manner since the main spars are still parallel over this length.

(3) The main front spar commences to sweep back after the above panel is past. The rear spar of this next panel can, however, be brought into line with the rear spar of the centre three panels by stretching a line over the rear spar of these panels and parallel to it, and then adjusting the bracing of the next panel till its main spar forms a continuation of the rear main spar of the three centre panels.

This alignment of the rear spars may also be checked by dropping plumb-lines from the edge of the rear spar at different points along its length and sighting these to see that they are all truly in line.

When all the planes are quite true, they may be covered with fabric and doped. In some cases, however, it may be preferable to erect the machine in skeleton form before proceeding to cover the wings. Before putting on the fabric great care must be taken that all turnbuckles are fitted with keep wires and all nuts properly locked. In putting the fabric on it must only be stretched to a moderate degree, otherwise the shrinkage which occurs during the process of doping may deform the plane. It is of the utmost importance that the leading edge of the planes shall be of the correct profile or cross-section, as on this, in a large measure, depends the efficiency of the wings. If difficulty has been experienced previously due to the leading portion of the wing distorting or losing its profile, intermediate "riblets" or false ribs should be inserted between the front main spar and the leading edge of the plane between each pair of ordinary ribs. These give the fabric the centre support necessary.

Erection.—The fuselage is set up on two trestles in the normal position, with the datum line and opposite points on the upper surface of the top longerons horizontal. In those types of machine where the datum line corresponds with the axis of the fuselage (as in the B.E. type), this may be obtained by clamping a straight-edge or batten along the side of the fuselage with its upper edge coinciding with the "Centre Line" marks on the middle of the vertical struts.

A level is placed on this batten and the fuselage packed up on the trestles until the top of the batten is horizontal. Fuselages in which the datum line is parallel to the top longerons may be packed up into the correct position by levelling up the top longerons themselves. This latter method may be applied whether the longerons are straight and parallel to the "Datum Line" over the whole length of the fuselage, as in the Sopwith machines, or only at the front part of the fuselage, as in the Short and Avro types. It will generally be found that when the machine is set up with the datum line horizontal, the engine bearers are also horizontal.

The fuselage is now levelled up in the transverse direction by placing a level on the top longerons of the fuselage at right angles to the axis of the fuselage. When the fuselage is levelled in both directions it should be fixed quite firmly by clamping it to the trestles so as to prevent any accidental displacement.

A very simple type of level which greatly facilitates the process of setting up the fuselage and wings can be constructed out of two large glass tubes, the lower ends of which are connected by a long piece of rubber tubing, and whose upper ends are open to the atmosphere. This apparatus is filled with water to a point about halfway up the two glass tubes. Since the water will always find its own level in the two tubes, it is merely necessary to hold one of the tubes against each of the vertical struts at the opposite end of the fuselage, and then to adjust the trestles till the surface of the water in each tube coincides with the marks at the middle of the respective end struts. The axis of the fuselage will then be accurately horizontal, assuming that the fuselage has been itself trued up correctly.

The next operation is the erection of the landing chassis, the construction of which differs in almost every type of machine.

In truing this up, the adjustments which have to be most carefully checked are (a) that the skids are parallel to one another and symmetrical about the axis of the fuselage, and (b) that the angle at which they are inclined to the horizontal is correct.

Taking the B.E. chassis as an example, the construction is explained in Fig. 8.

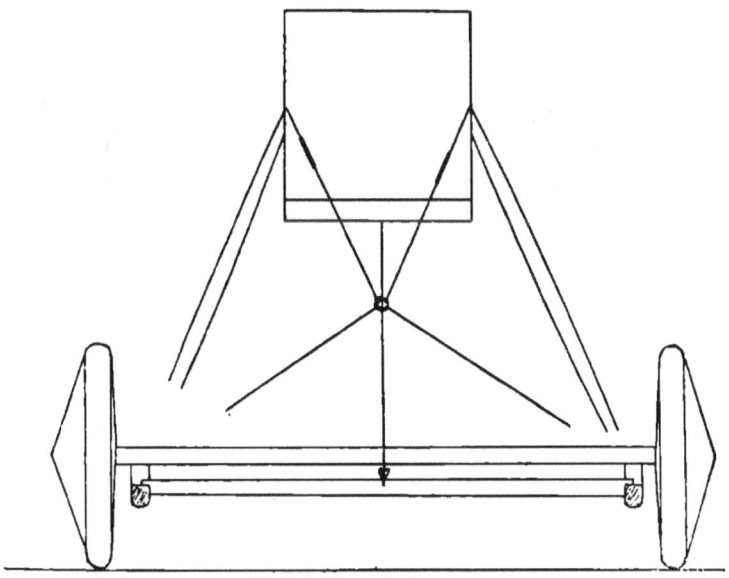

Fig. 8.

Before any attempt at erecting is commenced it should be seen that all the struts fit well home in their respective sockets, and also that each pair of corresponding struts are exactly the same and of the correct length.

The skids should also be placed alongside each other and checked for symmetry as regards the positions of their various fittings for mounting the undercarriage.

The skid struts are then fitted into their sockets on the skids and the whole lifted into place and packed up as nearly as possible in their true position under the fuselage.

To facilitate the erection of the under-carriage, two pieces of wood, cut to the correct length, are fixed as distance pieces between the two skids, one near the front end, and the other near the rear of the skid. These distance pieces hold the skids parallel to one another, and at the correct distance apart.

The distance between the skids is now accurately bisected along these distance pieces, and the bisecting points marked with a hard pencil. These bisecting points between the skids are now brought approximately under the centre line of the fuselage and jury wiring inserted in the under-carriage structure so as to hold it in position.

A plumb-line should now be dropped from each end of the fuselage, and immediately under the centre line of the fuselage ; the skids are then moved by adjusting the jury wiring till the bisecting points on their distance pieces come in the direct line between these two plumb-lines. This is checked by sighting, but in addition it is also advisable to drop plumb-lines from the centre line of the fuselage immediately above the skid distance pieces.

The actual bracing wires of the chassis are now inserted and tautened up, the alignment of the distance pieces accurately checked, and finally, the distance pieces between the skids are removed.

With regard to the angle of inclination of the skids to the ground, this should be tested for each skid most carefully. If found to be incorrect, it will be necessary to take down the chassis and again check over the length of the struts.

After this, the engine can be got into position and trued up. After levelling up the engine bearers, plumb-lines should be dropped from the fore and aft ends of the crankshaft, and these sighted with a line dropped from the rudder post. If these plumb-lines are all in the same straight line, the thrust of the propeller will lie somewhere in the vertical plane passing through the axis of the machine.

Erection of Main Wings.—The erection of the main wings can now be commenced.

The centre section of the top plane must be erected and trued up before anything further is attempted. The struts are first checked for length, from the drawing, and are then erected in their sockets on the upper side of the fuselage. The centre section of the plane is placed in position on top of these struts. and the necessary bracing wire inserted for this centre structure.

In most English machines the struts supporting the centre section are all truly vertical when the fuselage datum line is horizontal. This greatly assists the truing up of the centre section. The struts are brought vertical by means of a plumb-line, the bracing wires to this centre structure being adjusted as necessary. The centre fore-and-aft line of the centre plane section should now lie vertically over the centre line of the fuselage. In the case of some American machines, the struts are symmetrically inclined fore and aft, and also inwards towards the axis of the fuselage. In this case it is necessary to bisect accurately. The distance between the tops of the forward and aft struts on each side of the centre panel is, in this case, accurately bisected, and the middle points marked. From each of these points a plumb-line is dropped; then the fore-and-aft inter-strut wiring is adjusted until these lines come exactly midway between the bottoms of the struts on the upper longerons of the fuselage. The inward splay of the struts is next checked by a plumb-line from the side of the centre panel alongside each centre panel strut. The transverse inter-strut wiring is then adjusted till the splay of each separate pair of centre plane struts is the same. The centre line of the centre plane should then lie vertically over the centre line of the fuselage. This can be checked by plumb-lines.

In a few types of machines the centre section struts are inclined forward, and to check their slope it will be necessary to drop a plumb-line from each extremity of the leading edge of the centre section. If the stagger of the struts is incorrect, the incidence wires should be adjusted until the plumb-lines come vertically over the correct points previously marked on the two longerons of the fuselage, as obtained from the working drawings.

Great care must be taken to ensure that the angle of incidence of the centre section is exactly correct, since, if it is not so, it will be found after the machine is finally erected that the whole of the top plane is out of truth. The angle of incidence of the centre panel should therefore be checked; if it is found to be incorrect, the fault will probably be found in the length of the supporting struts from the top of the fuselage or the position of these strut sockets. These should, therefore, be most carefully re-checked before commencing to erect.

The bottom planes can now be erected into their approximately true positions, the inner ends being connected up to their respective sockets or fittings on the sides of the fuselage, and the outer ends supported on trestles. The upper planes are then ready for erection. The lengths of the interplane struts, and their fit into their respective sockets on the planes must be checked.

A scaffold is erected above the lower plane alongside each pair of interplane struts, and a man stationed alongside each strut.

The upper plane is then lifted to somewhere near its correct position, and the interplane struts fitted into their sockets on it. The whole is then lowered into position, and the lower ends of the struts entered into their respective sockets on the lower plane. The interplane bracing wires can now be attached to their respective fittings. In re-erecting a machine in which the exact lengths of the bracing wires are not definitely known, it is most convenient to fit temporary or jury interplane wiring at first, and to replace this later when the main planes are tuned up and the correct lengths of wire known. If, however, the lengths of the wires are known, this step is unnecessary.

Another method of erection sometimes adopted is to erect the whole main cell completely on the ground, wire it up, and afterwards lift it up and attach it to the fuselage as a complete unit.

The main cells have now to be trued up with regard to the dihedral angle, angle of incidence, stagger, &c.; these operations must be carried out in a definite order.

Truing up the Main Planes.—The first operation consists in getting the leading edges of the upper main planes into the correct positions relative to the axis of the fuselage.

The wings must be so placed that they are symmetrical about the axis of the fuselage, and in addition their leading edges must be given the correct "sweep back" (if any) relative to the centre section. A swept-back wing is very rare in British machines, and in general the leading edges of the wings are perpendicular to the axis of the fuselage.

The checking of the above characteristics of the wings necessitates two separate operations. In the first place a steel tape is stretched from the centre of each of the outer front strut sockets in turn to the centre of the rudder post. If the distances between these points as shown on the tape are equal, then the wings are symmetrical about the axis of the fuselage (*see* Fig. 9) in a horizontal plane.

Previous to checking the symmetry of the wings it should be ascertained that the corresponding strut sockets on the main spars are at an equal distance from the centre line of the fuselage, and are at corresponding points on the width of the main spars.

Secondly, if there is no "sweep back" to the wings, their alignment should be checked, since the two wings may be symmetrically placed on each side of the axis of the fuselage, and yet not be perpendicular to the axis of the fuselage.

This is best done by hanging plumb-lines against the leading edge at the inner and outer ends of each wing. By sighting along these four lines it can at once be seen whether the wings are in true alignment. If on checking the position of the wings in the foregoing manner it is found that either or both are not in the correct position, it will be necessary to plane a small amount off one end of the wooden box ribs forming the outside of the centre section, or off the main plane where it abuts the centre section. In practice, a small piece of packing may be inserted temporarily, and the thickness of this adjusted until the wings are brought square, and the correct amount may then be taken off the box rib at the end of the wing section.

When the upper plane is true the next operation is to get the lower plane parallel to the upper one. This is done by checking the stagger of the planes.

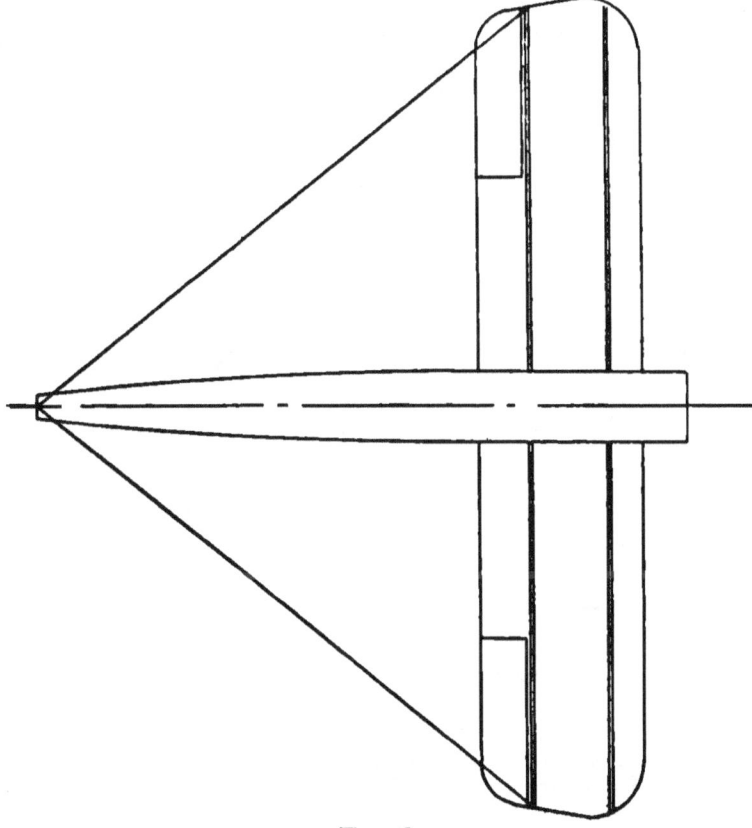

Fig. 9.

Stagger.—The stagger is the horizontal distance that the top plane projects in front of the bottom plane when the datum line of the fuselage is horizontal. This is checked directly by dropping plumb-lines from various points along the leading edge of the upper plane, and measuring the horizontal distance from this line to the leading edge of the bottom plane. (*See* Fig. 10.)

At the inner end of the planes the stagger is fixed by the position of the strut socket.

A line should be dropped from the leading edge of the top plane at the inner end and the stagger measured. This operation should be repeated at several points along the length of the planes, in order to make certain that the stagger of the top plane is uniform over the whole span of the machine.

If the stagger is not correct then the lower plane is not symmetrically placed relative to the fuselage, and the inner end of the lower planes will require planing in exactly the same manner as that described above for bringing the upper plane symmetrical to the axis of the fuselage.

The front spar must next be set up to the correct dihedral angle by means of adjusting the anti-lift wires between the main interplane struts. The incidence wiring should be left as slack as possible during this operation, so as not to interfere with any adjustments made on the anti-lift wire.

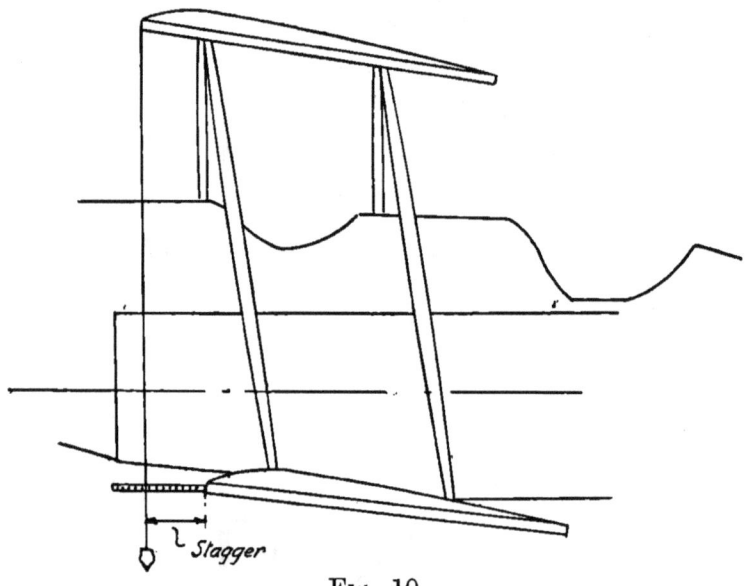

Fig. 10.

Dihedral Angle.—This is defined as the angle at which the spars of the wings are inclined to the horizontal when the machine is in normal flight (*see* Fig. 11). The most convenient

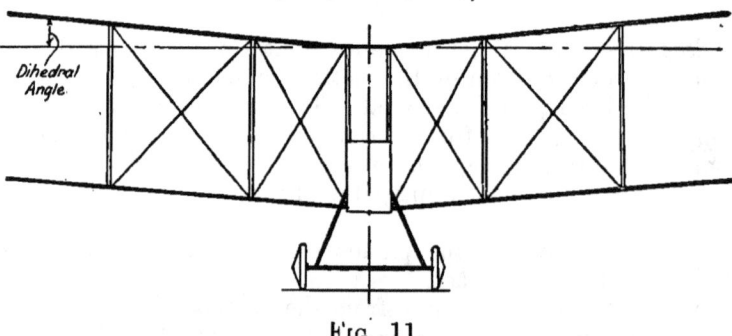

Fig. 11.

method of checking this is by means of a dihedral board. This board is cut to the correct dihedral angle, and, consequently, if one of its sides be placed on a main spar of the wing, the other side of the board will be horizontal if the spar is at its correct dihedral angle (*see* Fig. 12).

This dihedral board is placed on top of the wing's front spar, and the anti-lift bracing wires are adjusted until the upper edge of the board becomes horizontal, as shown by a level. When this edge of the board is level, the spar will be inclined at the correct angle to the horizontal. When the dihedral angle of the main planes is zero, the latter can be adjusted to their true horizontal positions by applying the water-level direct to the main spar itself.

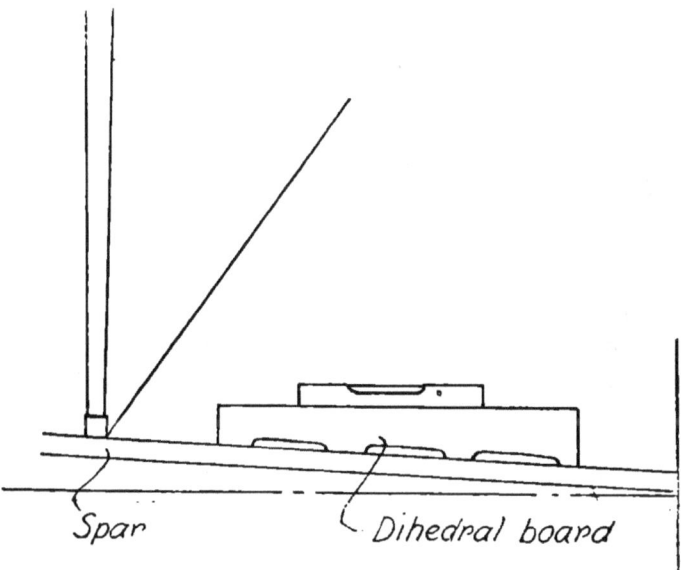

Fig. 12.

The rear spar should now be set up in an exactly similar manner, by adjusting its own anti-lift wires. If the truing up with the dihedral board is performed with care, the angle of incidence should now be correct everywhere along the planes at the end of this operation.

Angle of Incidence.—In workshop practice the angle of incidence of a wing surface is defined as the angle that, when the machine is in its normal flight attitude, the chord of the lower surface of the plane makes with the horizontal. For convenience in the erecting shop it is usually given in terms of Fig. 13, *i.e.*, the vertical distance between the respective levels of the leading and trailing edges of the wing's under surface.

In order to check the incidence of the lower main planes, a wooden batten is placed vertically, with its lower end on the floor and its upper end in contact with the leading edge of the lower plane.

A straight-edge is then placed with its upper edge in contact with the trailing edge of the plane, and is then brought up horizontal by means of a level. Whilst in this position it is steadied by being held to the vertical batten.

The distance AB can then be measured off directly with a rule.

This gives the incidence to which the wing is set. If the uniformity of the angle of incidence along the plane is merely being checked, the following method should be employed.

At about four places along the length of each of the planes a piece of string is tied right round the plane. This string will follow the contour of the upper surface of the wing, but at the lower side it will coincide with the chord of the under surface.

If the incidence of the wing is the same all along its length, *i.e.*, the machine is one in which there is no wash-out on the wings, its truth can at once be seen by sighting along the strings; they should all be parallel to one another.

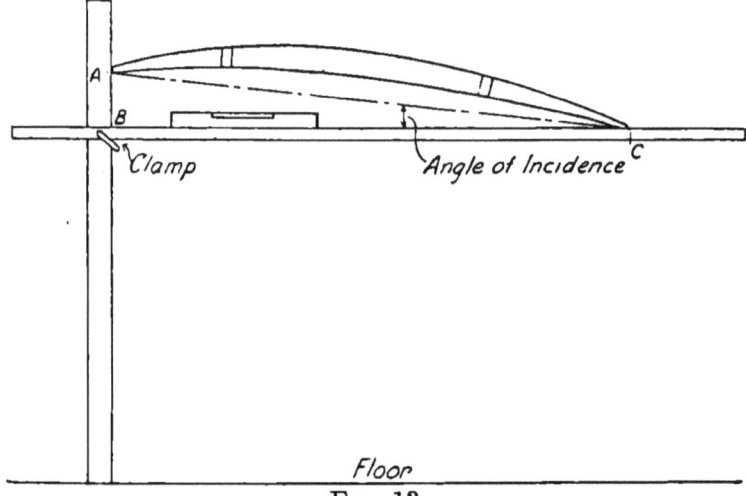

Fig. 13.

In truing up a wing the angle of incidence should first be carefully measured at the inner end of the planes, where the incidence is fixed by the position of the main spar sockets, in the fuselage; then, working outwards, the incidence should be checked at various points along the length of the plane to see that it is uniform.

As a final check, strings should be put round the plane at various points, and these sighted in the manner already explained.

If the angle of incidence is found to be incorrect at any point, it should be corrected by adjusting the anti-lift wires to the rear spar at that point, and on no account by adjusting the incidence wiring, which does not in reality control the incidence.

The lower plane should now be in truth, and, if the struts are all of correct length, the upper plane also. The incidence of this should be checked in the same way as that of the lower plane.

The lift wires are now carefully adjusted to the correct tension, and finally the incidence wires should all be tautened up correctly.

To adjust the ailerons, battens are held tangential to the camber of the upper and lower surfaces of the wings just in front of the aileron hinge, and the aileron should be fixed midway between these (*see* Fig. 14). When fitting the aileron

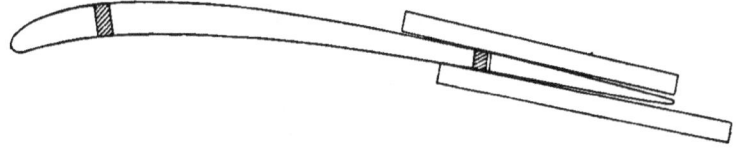

Fig. 14.

control cables the ailerons are packed up to a position about ¼-in. below the mean position shown in Fig. 14. The exact amount will vary with different machines and is a matter of experience. This is done by means of a tee batten (*see* Fig. 15). The control column or wheel is held in its neutral position, and the control wires are adjusted to be just taut with the ailerons in this position.

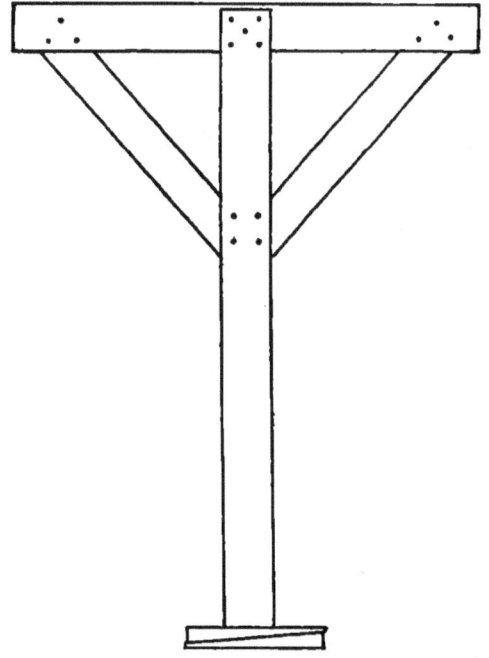

Fig. 15.

The Tail Plane.—The exact angle of incidence of the tail plane is generally obtained by actual flight and is fixed definitely according to the flying balance of each individual machine. The centre of the tail plane is set up to the correct angle of incidence on the fuselage, ignoring, for the time being, its outer ends. The plane must be placed so that its main spar is perpendicular to the axis of the fuselage. This is tested by measuring the distances of the extremities of the tail plane from some point on the axis of the fuselage, in a similar manner to that used in setting up the leading edge of the main planes symmetrically with the axis of the machine. The rear spar is then brought horizontal with a level, and secured in this position. The front spar or leading edge of the tail plane is then treated in exactly the same manner and secured into position by the stay rods or wiring.

Check the incidence of the plane and then set up the elevator flaps in the same manner as that employed for the ailerons, adjusting the control wires so as to be just taut when the control column is vertical.

Check the movement of all controls up and down, seeing that the range of movement is correct in both directions.

Put the rudder bar in its midship position, and block it there. Fit the rudder wires and make them just taut when the rudder is neutral, and check the rudder movement to right and left, to obtain its travel and also to see that sufficient slackness has been allowed in the control wires.

Note on the Use of Spirit Levels.—The usual method of using a level is to place it on the spar, &c., and then adjust until the bubble is in the centre of the tube.

As the ordinary type of spirit level is usually very inaccurate, this may lead to erroneous results.

The proper method of using a spirit level is to mark with a soft lead pencil the position of one end of the bubble and then to reverse the level and see if the end of the bubble still coincides with the mark. If it does correspond, the spar, or whatever is being tested, will be accurately level.

The greatest care must be taken that the level whenever it is employed is held perfectly square in the transverse direction, otherwise false readings may result.

CHAPTER III.

"Pusher" Type Machines.

Maurice Farman (1913) *Machines.*—The first operation consists in truing up the upper and lower main planes themselves. These are in turn assembled and placed on trestles. They are now adjusted by means of the internal drift wiring, until the main spars are in true alignment. This is checked either by sighting along the spars or by getting a line stretched along exactly as explained for "Tractor" type machines.

Erecting the Main Cell.—The positions of the strut sockets on the top and bottom planes is checked for symmetry, and in addition the struts are to be checked for length.

When the planes are in truth, the centre section of the lower plane is got into a horizontal position on trestles and is packed up until the chord of the lower surface and each main spar are perfectly horizontal, this being checked by means of a level.

The struts are now erected in their sockets and the centre section of the upper plane got into position, the whole being wired up with *temporary* bracing wires.

The wiring is now adjusted until the struts are all perfectly vertical, as shown by a plumb-line, and the main spars of the lower centre section are 9 mm. higher at the point where they are cut by the plane of symmetry than at the ends. This hog or arch in the two main spars is obtained by tautening up the lift and checking the anti-lift bracing wires in the two inner panels. The adjacent sections of the main cell are then assembled on to the centre section, and the whole wired up and adjusted in the same manner, the chord of the lower surface and each of the main spars being horizontal, and the struts truly vertical. Proceeding outwards the whole of the main cell is erected and trued up in the same manner.

Finally a line should be stretched across the span of the wings, between the struts situated at opposite ends of the main cell, at a distance of, say, $\frac{1}{4}$ inch above the spar. If the adjustments have been correctly made this will be at a uniform distance above the spar right across the planes, except at the centre section where the spar is arched to take the weight of the nacelle, engine, &c.

Erection of Tail Cell.—The tail cell is erected in exactly the same manner as the main cell, but the main spars are not hogged at the centre of the tail. The upper and lower planes are first trued up; the lower plane is then placed on trestles with the chord of the lower surface horizontal, and the whole cell is assembled with temporary wiring which is adjusted until all the struts are perfectly vertical.

Tail Booms.—These should all be laid out on the floor and checked for length, the position of the sockets, &c. They are then assembled with the cross struts and the bracing wires inserted. The whole is then erected, suitably supported on chocks and fitted on to the main and tail cell units. The centre panels of the tail boom unit is now trued up by tramelling its diagonals and adjusting its bracing wires until the latter are equal. The two outside panels are now trued up, the bracing wires being adjusted until the booms are straight and in true alignment, this being tested either by sighting or by running a line along the booms.

The main cell and the tail cell should now be in their correct positions relative to each other. This is now checked by running a line through from the front strut of the main cell at a height of ·965 metres (3 ft. 2 ins.) from the top of the main spar to the front strut of the tail cell at a height of ·715 metres (2 ft. 4·1 ins.) from the top of its main spar. This line should then cut the rear strut of the main cell at a height of ·94 metre (3 ft. 1 in.) above the top of the rear spar. Should it cut this strut at any other point the length of all the tail boom members should be re-checked, and, if necessary, the tail boom wiring readjusted till this measurement is correct. The nacelle may now be got into position and secured, and the under-carriage assembled.

Erection of Under-Carriage.—The vertical distance from the bottom of the front spar to the top of the skid is 1·06 metres (3 ft. 5·7 ins.) and from the bottom of the rear spar to the top of the skid is 1·05 metres (3 ft. 5·3 ins.). The under-carriage is erected on exactly the same principle as that adopted for the tractor.

Angle of Incidence.—The machine has now to be set up in the flying position. This is effected by packing up the tail of the machine until the engine bearers in the nacelle are perfectly horizontal.

The incidence of the main and tail planes is now checked in the same manner as already explained in connection with tractor machines.

The incidence of the plane has already been defined as the vertical distance from the leading edge of the plane to a horizontal straight-edge in contact with the trailing edge. The incidence of the tail plane checked in this way should be 3·5 cms. (1·38 ins.). The incidence of the centre section and the whole of the right-hand wing is uniform and equal to 9 cms. (3·54 ins.). In the Maurice Farman machine the left-hand wing is arranged with a greater angle of incidence than the right-hand wing, the increased lift so obtained being employed to produce a moment which balances the propeller torque. The increased incidence is obtained by sloping the rear spar of this wing slightly downwards by means of the rear anti-drift wires. When correctly adjusted the angle of incidence at the extreme left-hand strut should be 10·5 cms. (4·13 ins.), at No. 2 strut 10 cms. (3·94 ins.), and at No. 3 strut 9·5 cms. (3·74 ins.). The last operation consists in replacing the temporary wiring by the final bracing wires, when the correct lengths of the latter have been found. The incidence wiring is finally tautened up correctly.

The erecting and adjustment of control gear, &c. is effected in exactly the same way as in tractor type machines, with the exception of the elevator. If a front elevator is provided, then the top surface of this should be horizontal when the tail or rear elevator is fixed in its neutral position.

"America" Type Curtiss Flying Boats.

Hull.—The boat is levelled in the transverse direction carefully. The fore-and-aft position of the hull is not of such great importance, as the relation of the planes and the hull in this direction are fixed by the short wing bases which form part of the hull itself, and cannot therefore be adjusted.

Main Planes.—These are assembled on trestles and checked for truth by diagonal measurements in the usual manner, the adjustments being made by means of the internal bracing wires. The joint plates and sockets are then fitted and the struts checked over for length, fit into sockets, &c.

The floats should be temporarily fixed in place on the lower planes before erecting, a centre line being marked on the float and this made to come vertically under a centre line marked on the rib. Final adjustments are made after the planes have been trued up.

Lower Planes.—These are got into place on the boat, being packed up into position at a dihedral angle of 1° 45′, *i.e.*, 6 inches rise measured on the distance between the centre of the outer strut and the point where the plane abuts the short wing base which is built into the hull.

A trestle is placed near the outer strut and the wing packed up at the inner end. It is then slipped into position and bolted up to the socket which should have been previously fixed in place.

Centre Section.—The centre section is next erected. The centre struts are first got into position. The engine bearer struts and engine bearers are now connected up on the bench, and the horizontal cross struts attached to them. These units are now picked up and dropped into the fore and aft engine strut bottom sockets, and at the same time the horizontal strut is pushed into the socket on the centre strut. The centre section of the top plane is now lifted up and got into place on the struts. Four men are required, one at each corner. Lastly the section is wired and trued up in the same manner as that described for a tractor centre plane section.

The truing up of the centre section is extremely important and must be most carefully carried out, as the truth of the whole machine depends on this.

The engine bearer struts are now to be squared up by overall diagonal measurement or by getting the struts vertical by means of a plumb-bob, the centre strut being neglected for the time being. The rear struts are set up in a similar manner.

The incidence of the centre section is now carefully checked. If incorrect, the lengths of the struts should be re-checked. It is necessary to make certain that the diagonal struts are vertical in the fore-and-aft direction and that the diamonds formed by the engine bearers and engine bearer struts do not bulge forward at the engine bearers. A slight camber or hollow aft may be tolerated, provided it is very small, as the engine thrust tends to cause it to bend in the opposite direction in flight. The truth of this diamond formed by the engine bearers and the engine bearer struts, should be tested by trying whether the diagonals bisect. A plumb-line hung from the centre of the upper socket is the handiest method.

Erecting the Main Planes.—At each end of the plane scaffolds are erected across the lower plane at a convenient height, and cross boards placed athwartships across these at the fore-and-aft sides of the plane. A man is required at each engine strut and outer strut. After the struts have been tried in their sockets for fit, the plane is lifted high enough to let the outer struts be slipped into the top sockets and made fast. The plane is next got into the inner joint plates, and bolted up. The outer struts are now lowered into position in the bottom sockets. The inner struts should be eased into the sockets and made fast, and finally the bottom end of the outer strut is secured.

The temporary wiring is next got into place in all the bays, and the pylons erected, so as to be ready for the extensions.

The main planes are now ready for truing up.

Truing up the Main Planes.—The procedure is similar to that employed in truing up ordinary tractor machines.

The alignment of the leading edges of the planes is first checked.

The flying wires are adjusted until the dihedral of the front and rear spars of the lower plane are correct (1·75-in.). The angle of incidence of the lower plane should now be uniform along the length of the plan; the actual value being $4\frac{1}{2}°$. If necessary the flying wires may need a final adjustment to correct this.

The upper plane is got into truth by getting the struts perfectly vertical with a plumb-line, and the angle of incidence is then checked. If this is found incorrect anywhere, the lengths of the struts must be re-checked.

Plane Extensions.—Suitable scaffolding is put up and the plane extensions erected. The plane is slid into the joint plates and bolted up, the wiring made fast both to the pylons and the lower plane wiring plate.

The incidence of the extension is then checked, and, if necessary, modified by altering the length of the wires from the pylon. The lift wires are then adjusted in the usual manner.

The ailerons may then be attached. The plane extensions should now be trued up in exactly the same way as the main planes.

When all is complete it is as well to test the main plane, extension, and centre section, for alignment across the whole span of the machine, by dropping plumb-lines at intervals over the leading edge of the lower plane and sighting along these.

The ailerons may be attached to the extension planes before erecting the latter, and the whole erected as a complete unit. If they are erected after the extensions are in place, the alignment of the extension should in this case be re-checked after the ailerons are attached.

Measurements are now taken for the length of the cables, and permanent bracing wires substituted for the temporary wiring. Care must be taken to see that no bay is left inadequately wired while this is proceeding, or distortion is certain and serious damage is likely to be done.

Fin.—This is fitted to the mortice on the hull, the front socket put on and also the clips attached to the boat, and finally the stays are fixed. The fin should be tested for plumb, both before and after fixing stays.

Tail Plane.—The tail plane is slipped over the fin and fixed to clips. The tail is set at right angles to the axis of the main struts, *i.e.*, set neutral at first. The stays should then be fixed. It is to be borne in mind that the exact final setting of the tail is experimental and depends on trial flight. It will in most cases differ slightly from boat to boat, even though they are of exactly the same design.

The rudder and elevators are next put in place. Both are to be wired before erection.

The tail plane should be parallel to the cellule. When the machine is in the flying position the incidence of the fixed plane should be as shown in Fig. . If in flight the machine pushes too much against the pilot, another degree more incidence should be put in the tail. If the pilot has to pull, a degree less of incidence should be given. The incidence can be altered by adjusting the steel quadrant on the front spar of the tail, and the four wires which pull from the middle of the front spar.

In horizontal flight, with the engine running full out, there should be a distinct pressure against the pilot's hand.

The axis of the motor is parallel to the line of flight, *i.e.*, when the main cellule struts are vertical the crank shaft is horizontal.

CAUDRON BIPLANE, G.4. TYPE.

Truing the Cellule.—The front spar of the top plane is set truly horizontal and in correct alignment.

The control lever should be set in a vertical position and fastened so as to be immovable.

The tail of the machine should be packed up until the cellule struts are exactly perpendicular.

The incidence measured between *the lower face of the front spar and the lower face of the back spar* should now be checked in this position.

Beneath the nacelle the spars should be level.

Above the left-hand skid the bottom of the back spar should be 12 mm. lower than the bottom of the front spar.

Above the right-hand skid the bottom of the back spar should be 12 mm. higher than the bottom of the front spar.

Under the right- and left-hand cellule struts both spars should be level; also the spars of the top plane extension.

In practice, if the struts are all of the correct length, it is only necessary to true the lower plane.

The tail booms and skids can now be trued. The left-hand side should be trued up first, then the right-hand side aligned with it.

The machine should be kept in the same position, *i.e.*, the main cellule strut vertical, and a batten placed on the back spar of the bottom plane.

When this batten is horizontal the top of the back skid should be 34·5 cm. below the bottom of the guide.

Two parts of the left-hand tail boom form a straight line. On the other hand the two parts of the right-hand tail boom form a line broken upwards at the large tail boom strut.

APPENDIX.

DIAGRAMS SHOWING THE METHOD OF TRUING UP DIFFERENT TYPES OF AEROPLANES AND SEAPLANES.

SOPWITH 1½ STRUTTER.
110 H.P CLERGET.

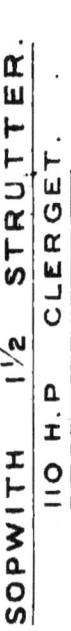

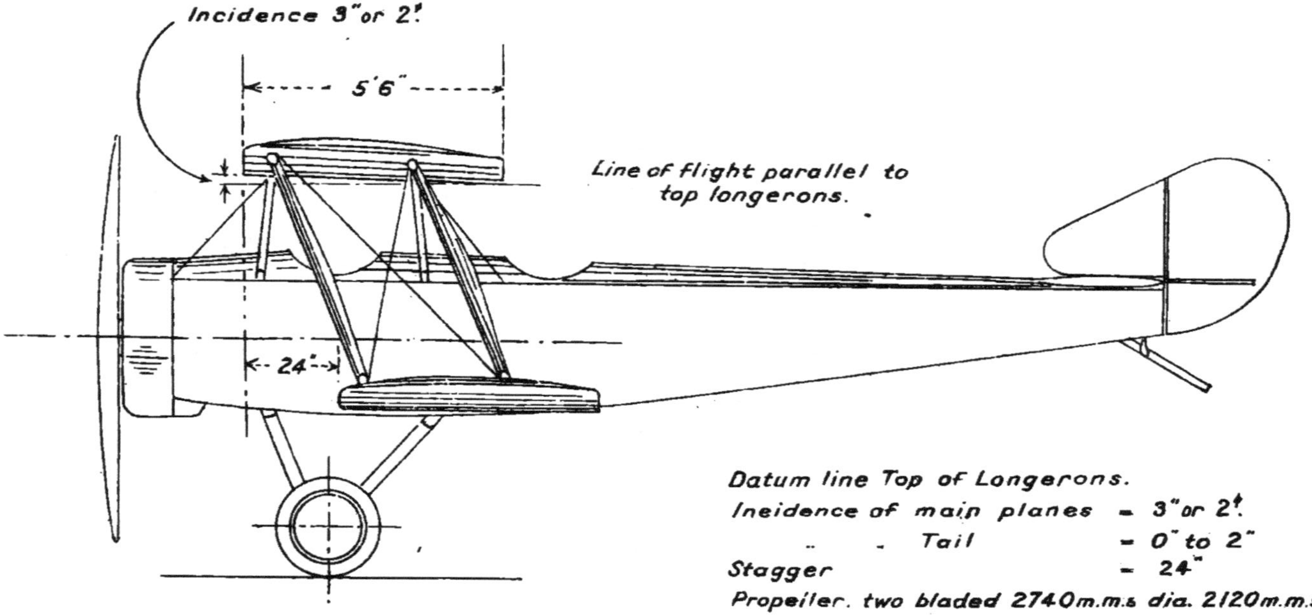

Incidence 3"or 2'.
5'6"
Line of flight parallel to top longerons.
24"

Datum line Top of Longerons.	
Ineidence of main planes	= 3"or 2'.
" " Tail	= 0" to 2"
Stagger	= 24"
Propeller. two bladed 2740m.m.s dia. 2120m.m.s pitch.	
Washout	= None
Throw back of wings.	= "
Set of Fin.	= "

4659.

Malby & Sons, Lith.

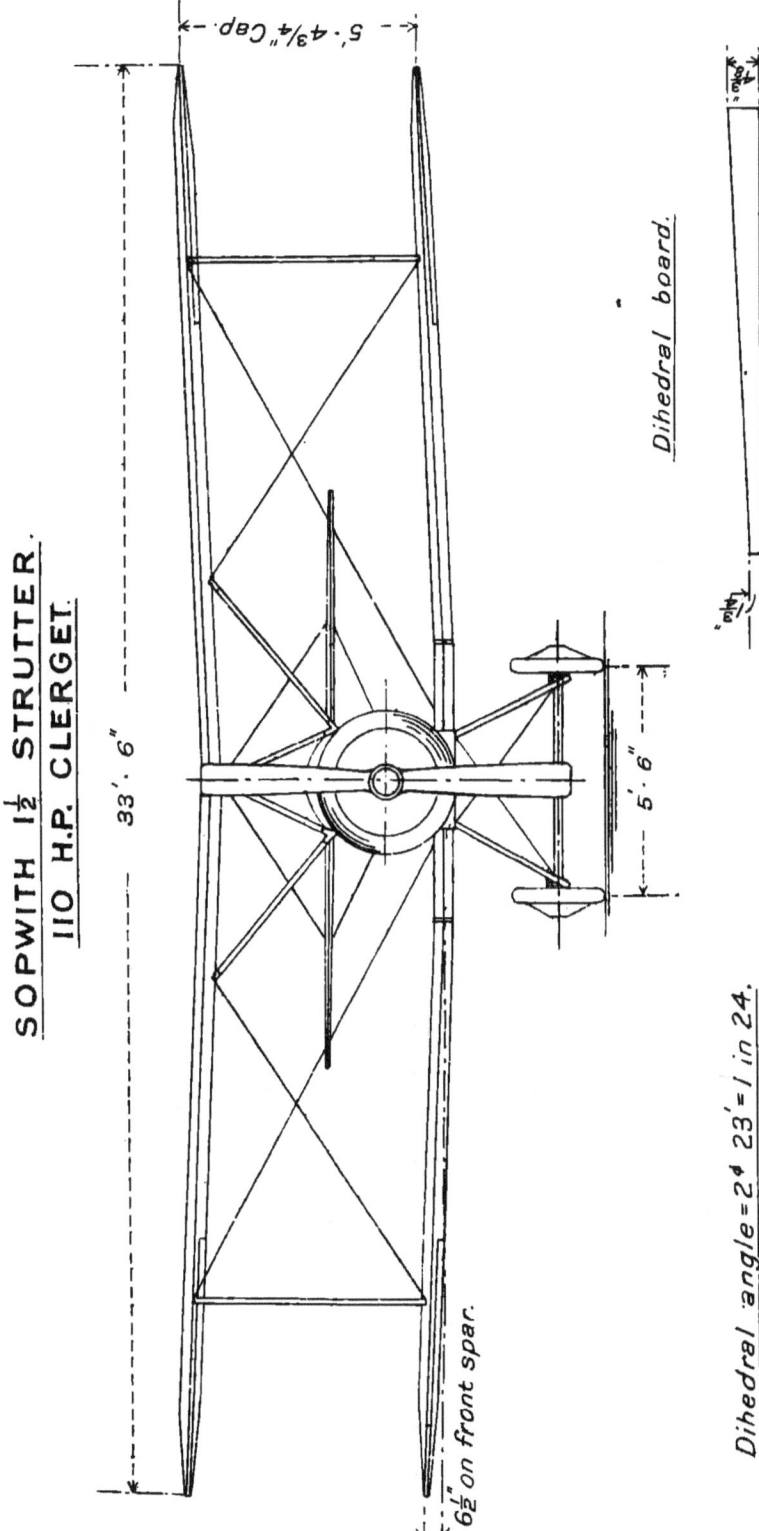

SOPWITH 2 SEATER.

SCOUT.
80 H.P. GNOME.
1051—74.

Incidence 3¼"
Stagger nil

5' 1½"

Line of flight parallel to top of Fusilage

Incidence of chord of main planes 3¼ inches.

Chord of tail plane parallel to top of Fusilage.

Datum Line — Top of Top Longerons.
Incidence of Chord of Main Planes 3¼ inches.
Wash out — Nil.
Stagger — Nil.
Incidence of Chord of Tail Planes Zero.
Throw back of Wings — Nil.
Set of Fin — Nil.
Struts of Main Cell. Forward Length 63 11/16" overall.
    "   "   Back   "   63⅝"
Propeller — Chauviere 2 blades 2·60m.dia. 1·60m. Pitch.

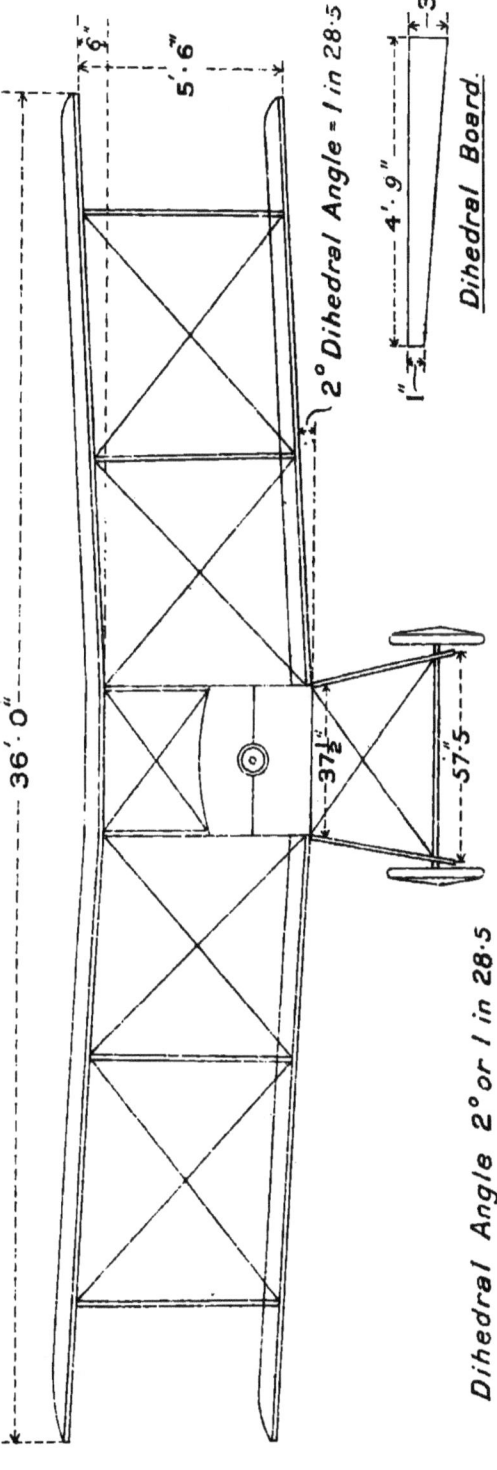

150 H.P. SOPWITH PUSHER.

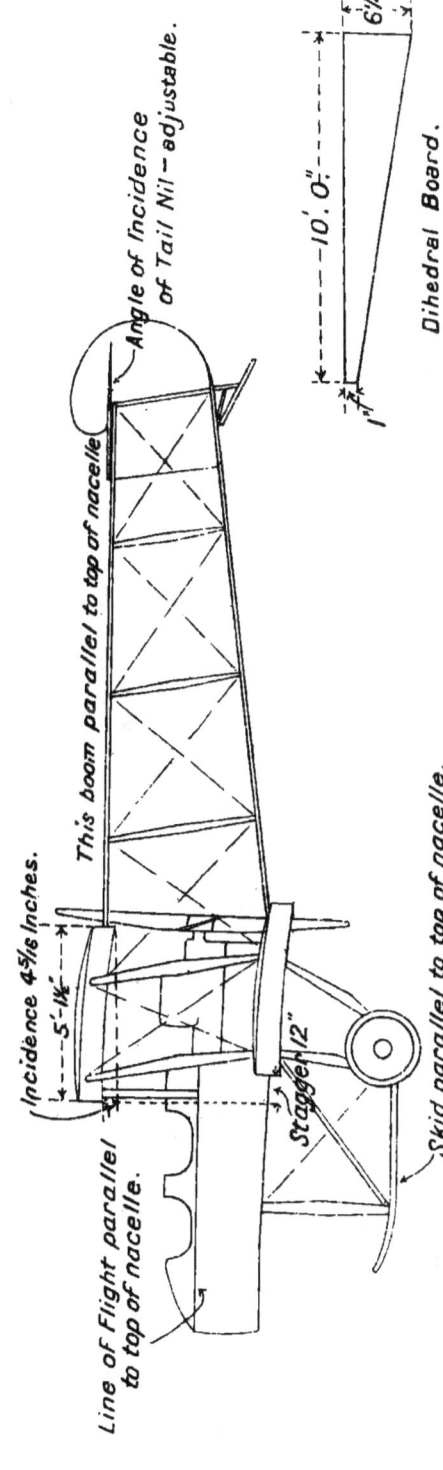

Line of Flight parallel to top of nacelle.
Incidence of Main Planes 4.5/16 Inches.
Wash out — Nil.
Stagger — 12"
Incidence of Tail Planes Nil — adjustable.
Throw back of Wings — Nil.
Set of Fin — Nil.

Dihedral angle 1 in 22·86
Skids parallel to top of nacelle.
Spacing of skids 4' 10" Centres.
Propeller fitted Laing 4 bladed. 2·9 m. dia. 2·0 m. Pitch.

SOPWITH SCHNEIDER CUP.
MACHINE 1436-47.

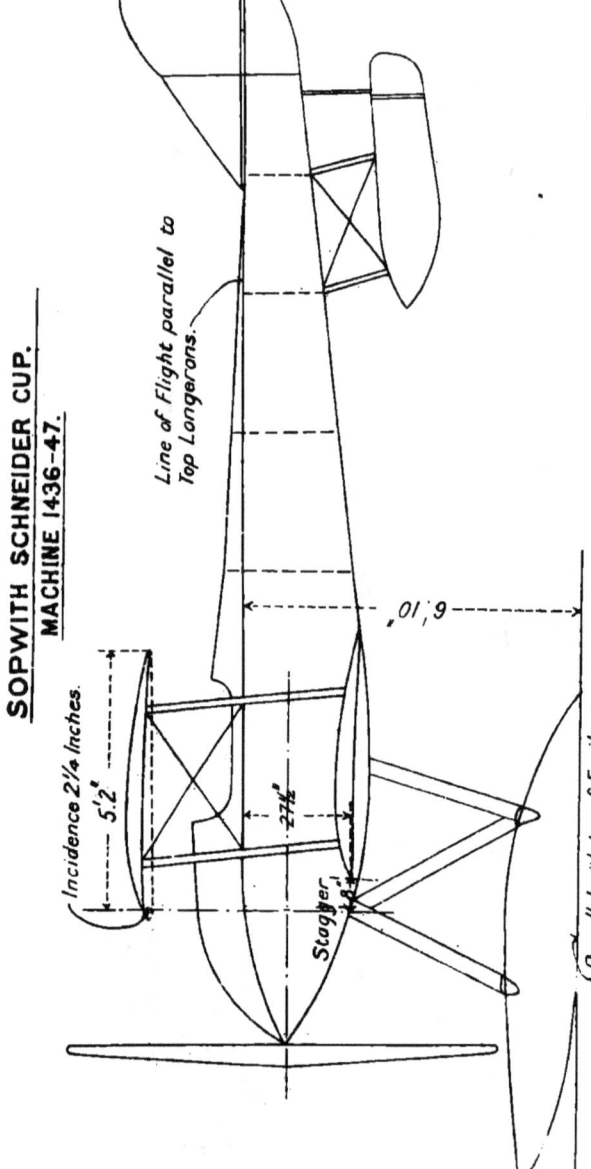

Line of Flight parallel to Top Longerons.

Incidence 2¼ Inches.
5'2"
Stagger 8"
27½"
6'10"
(Parallel with top of Fusilage.)

Datum Line Top of top of Longerons.
Incidence of Chord of Main Planes 2¼ inches.
Wash out — Nil.
Stagger 8"
Incidence of Chord of Tail Planes Zero degrees.
Throw back of Wings — Nil.
Set of Fin — Nil.
Struts of Main Cell Ford Struts overall 51⅞"
Aft. 5¼
Propeller Long 2 Blades 2·65 m. Diam 2·10 m. Pitch

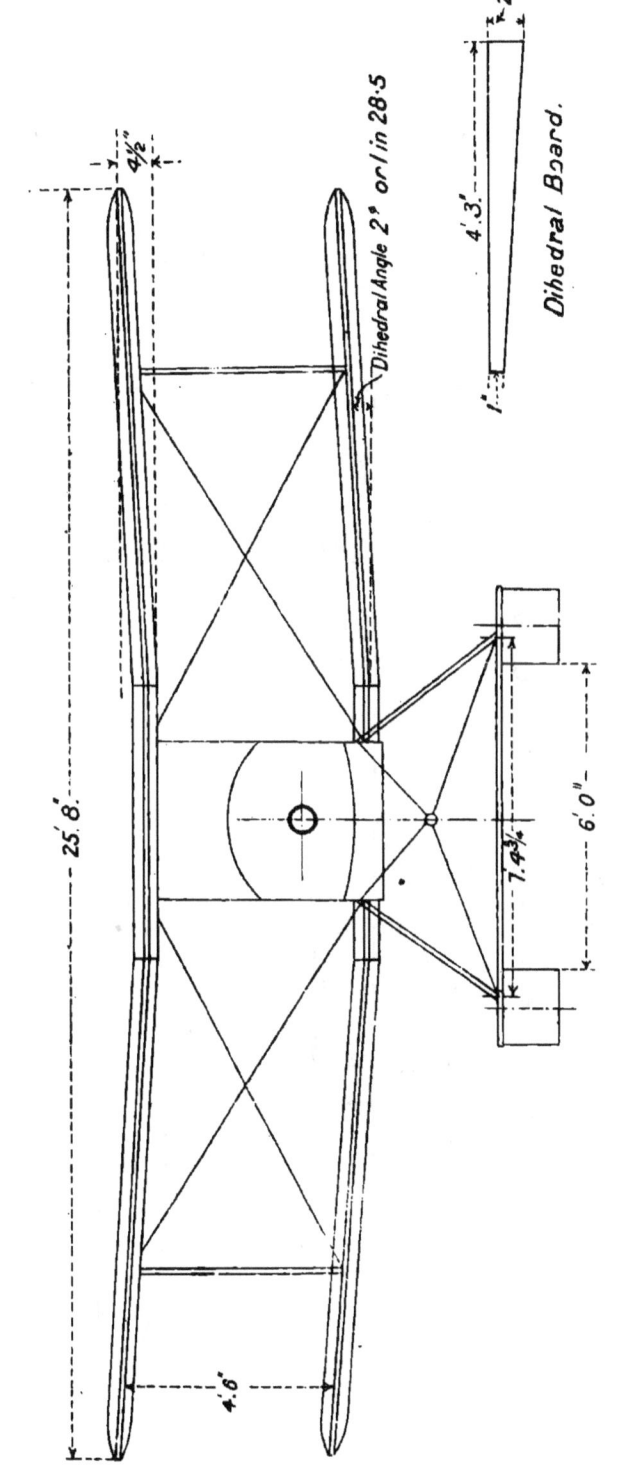

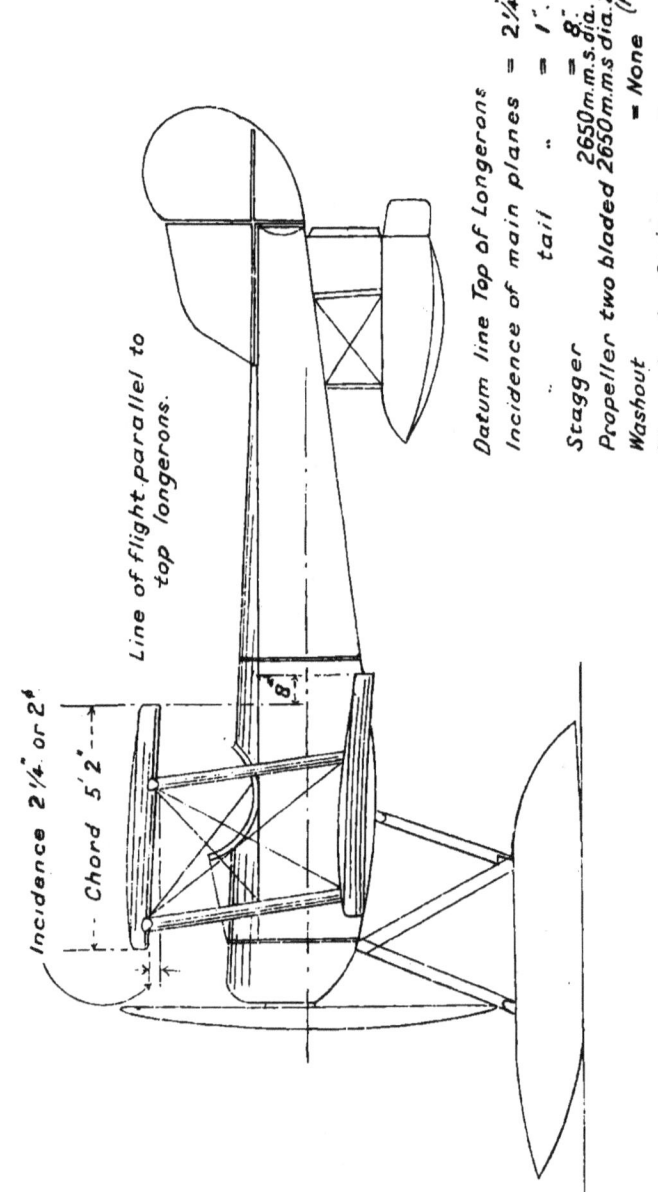

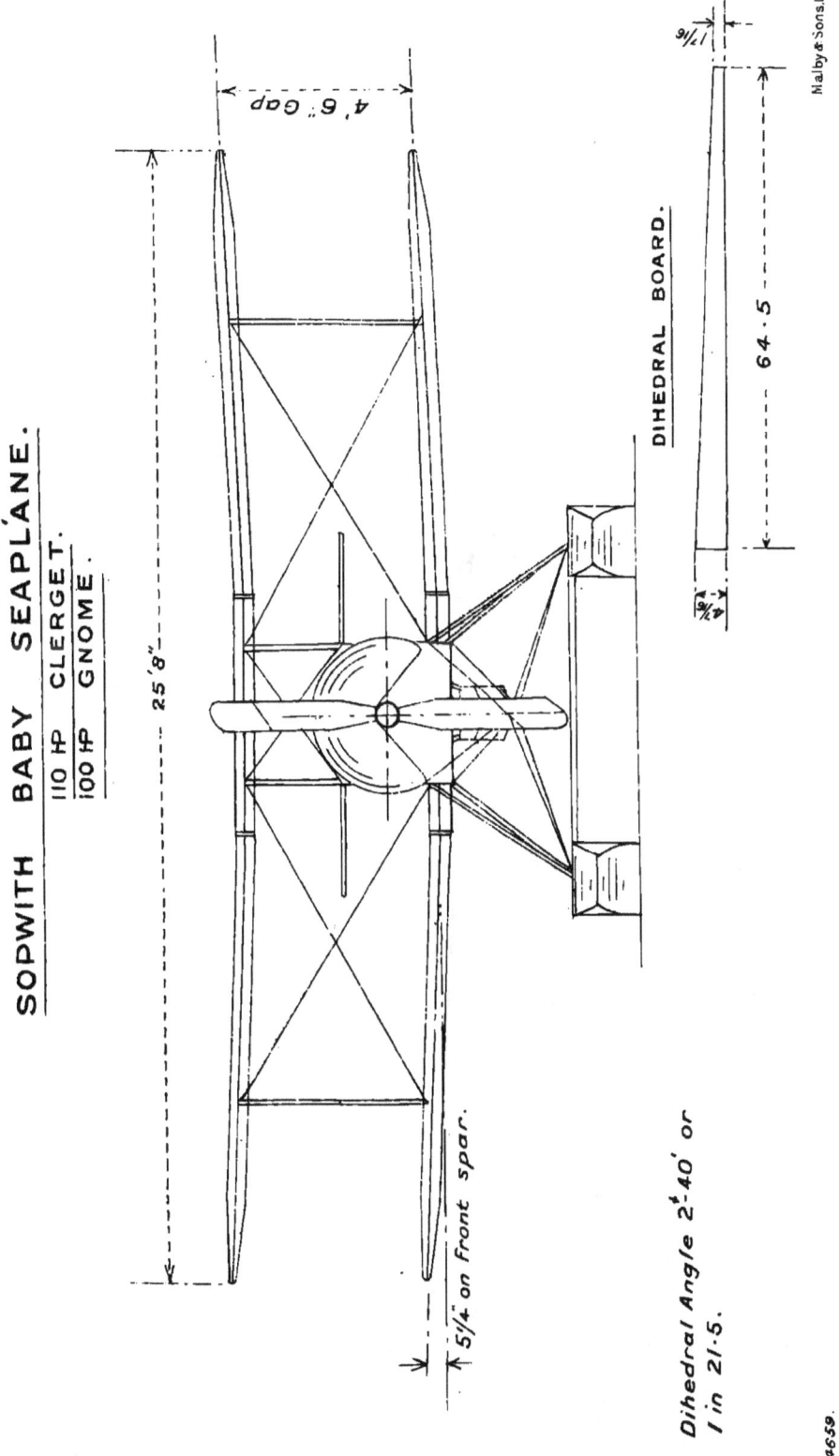

AVRO BIPLANE.
TYPE 504.

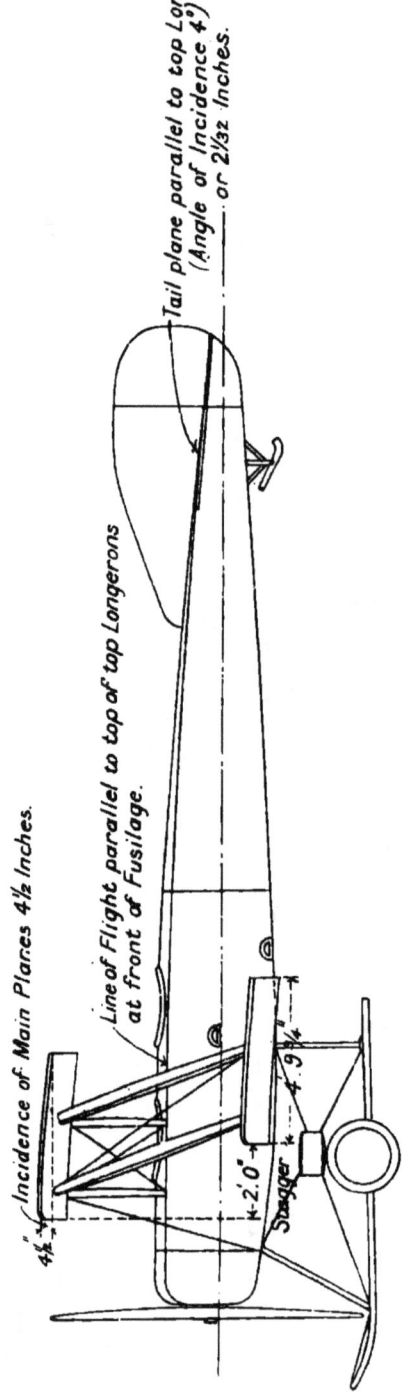

Line of Flight parallel to top Longeron at front part of Machine.
Incidence of Main Planes 4½ Inches.
Wash out — Nil. adjustments (lateral) made by washing in L.H. plane.
Stagger 2'.0".
Incidence of Tail Planes 2/32" or 4°.
Throw back of Wings — Nil.
Set of Fin — Perpendicular and parallel to line of Flight.
Propeller fitted "Avro" 9'.C." Dia. 6'.0". Pitch.

AVRO BIPLANE.
TYPE 504.

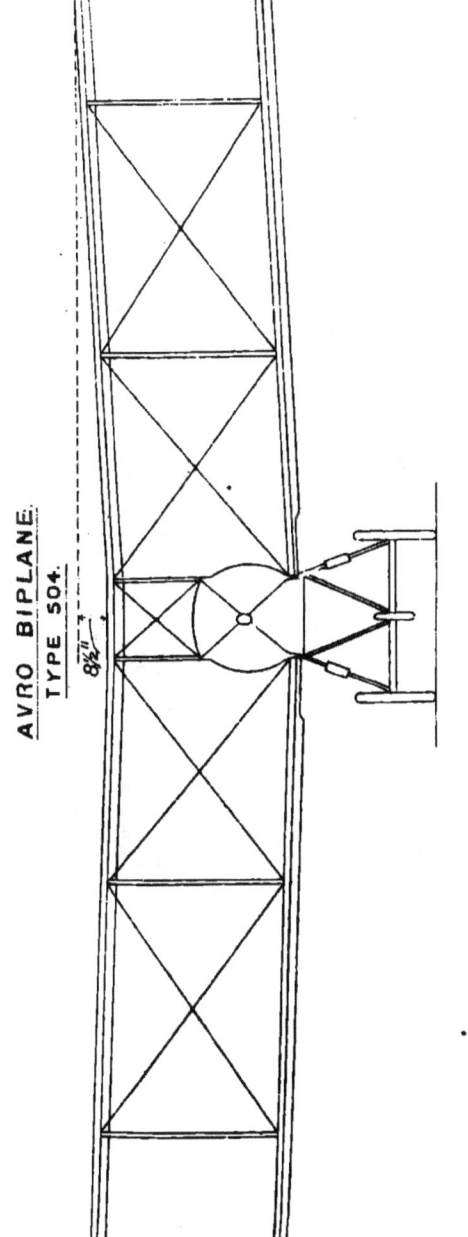

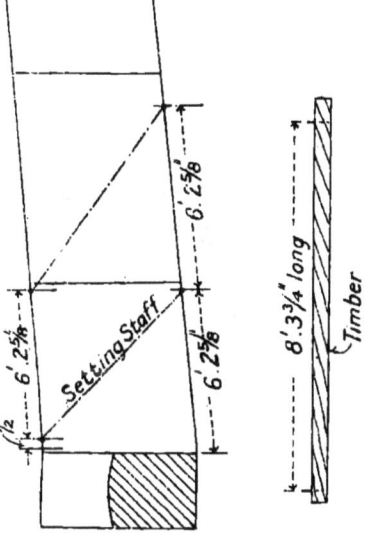

Dihedral 8½ inches can be Checked by Cord between Wing tips.

The dihedral angle is fixed by the Setting Staff shown.
This is used to Measure the distance between the points shown in the Sketch.
These points are marked on the Planes by means of small Aluminium Plates.

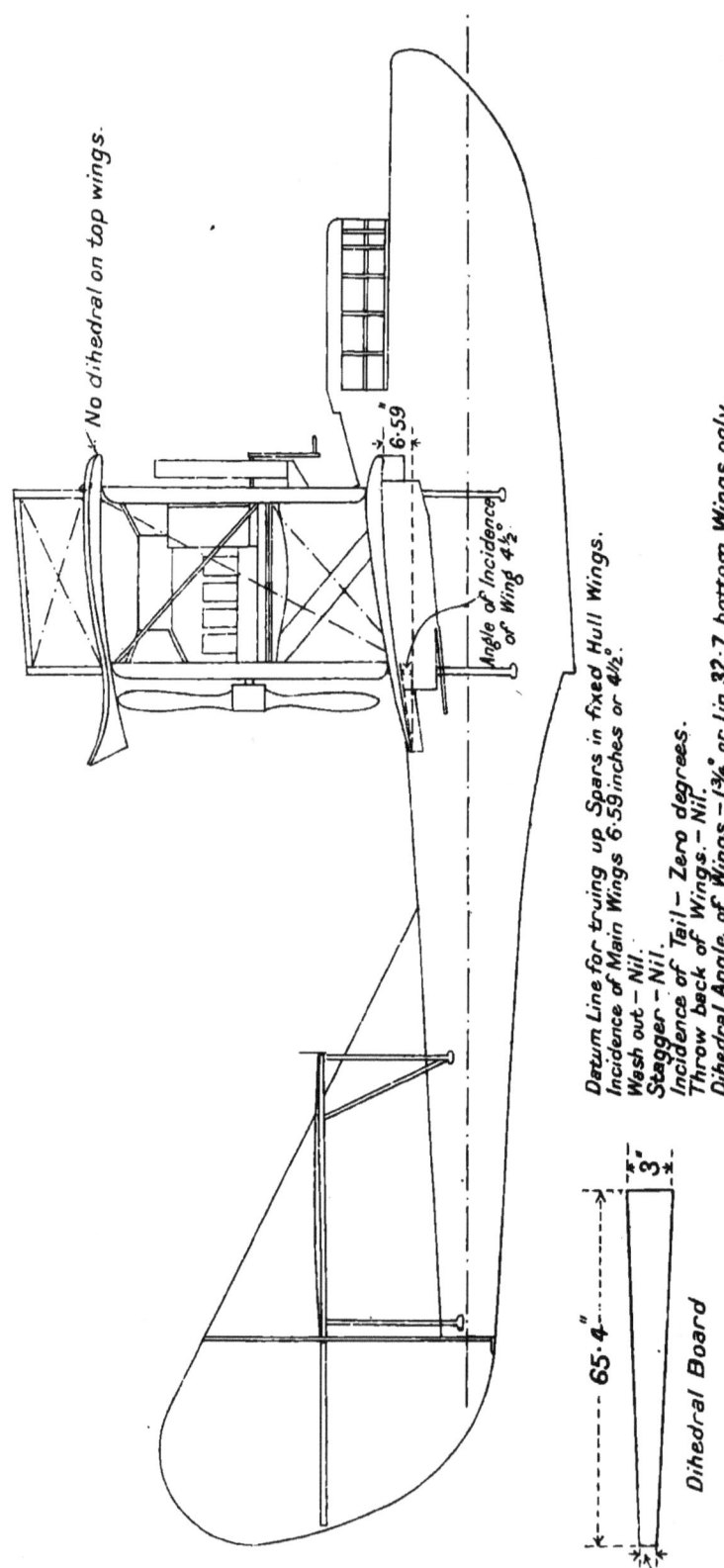

SHORT 150 H.P. SEAPLANE.

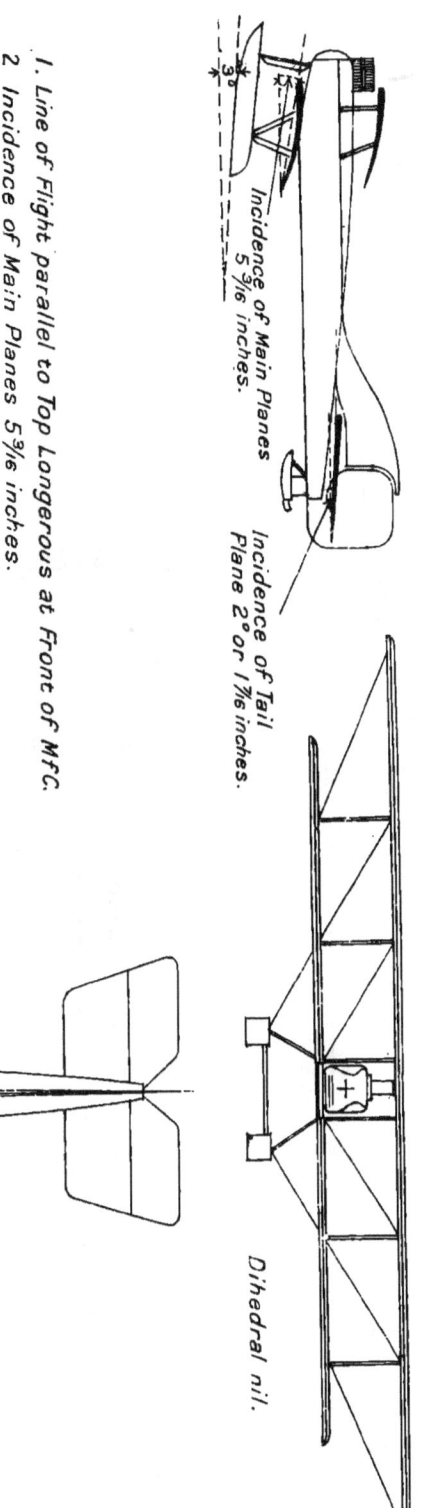

Incidence of Main Planes 5 3/16 inches.

Incidence of Tail Plane 2° or 1 7/16 inches.

Dihedral nil.

1. Line of Flight parallel to Top Longerous at Front of M.F.C.
2. Incidence of Main Planes 5 3/16 inches.
3. Wash out. nil.
4. Stagger. nil.
5. Incidence of Tail Plane 1 7/16 inches.
6. Throw back of Wings. nil.
7. Set of Fin. nil.
8. Angle of base of Floats 3°
9. Propellor Short Type 10'-4" diam. × 6'-8" mean pitch.

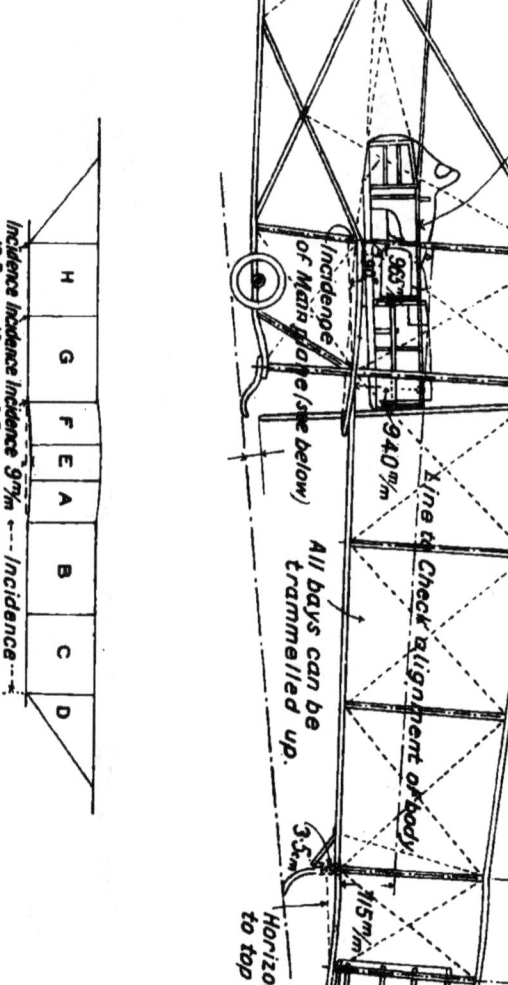

M. FARMAN MACHINE
(80 H.P. RENAULT)
WITH BIPLANE TAIL.

Maurice Farman, 1913 (80 h.p. Renault), with Biplane Tail.

LENGTHS OF STRUTS.

These Lengths are the Centre Lines of the Struts.

	Front.	Rear.
A	199·8 m/m	200·2 m/m.
B	,,	,,
C	,,	,,
D	190·8 m/m	191·2 m/m.
E	199·8 m/m	200·2 m/m.
F	,,	,,
G	,,	,,
H	190·8 m/m	191/2 m/m.

ERECTING.

At B and F angle XYZ = 90°.

Lower plane get B and F in horizontal line on trestles and struts B and F vertical (front and rear).

Tauten landing wires till centre portion of front and back spars are cambered 5 m/m.

Wing portion of planes:—

Port: Angle XYZ = 90° and both front and rear spars horizontal.

Starboard: Front spars horizontal.
Rear spars tuned by dihedral boards, viz.,
Port wing, 1 in.—416 up.

Front elevator horizontal in flying position and tail elevator forms continuation of the upper and lower surface of tail planes. Incidence as shown in diagram.

Incidence at A E F and B = 90 m/m.
,, ,, H = 100 m/m.
,, ,, G = 95 m/m.
,, ,, C = 85 m/m.
,, ,, D = 80 m/m.

N.B.— The incidence is taken between back and front spars and not from trailing edge.

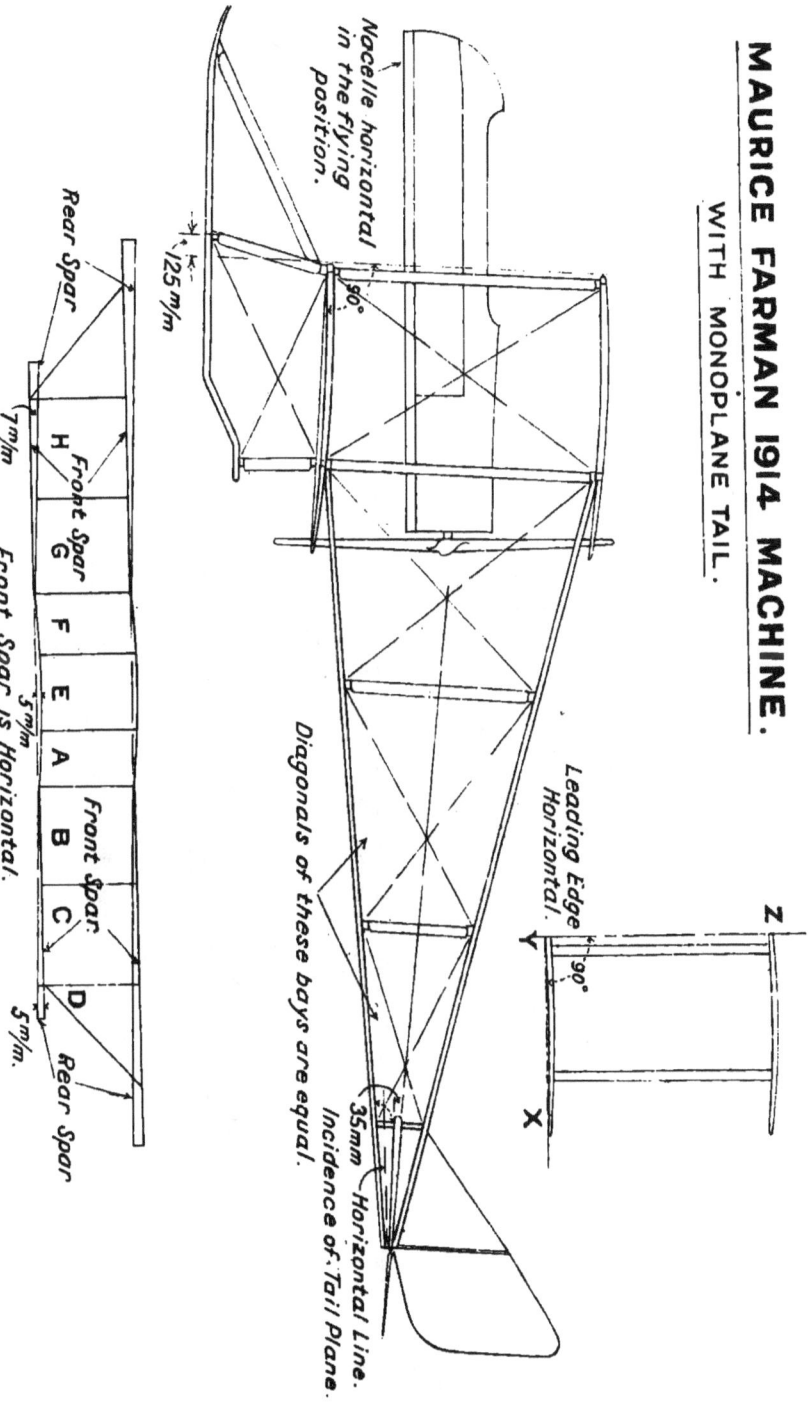

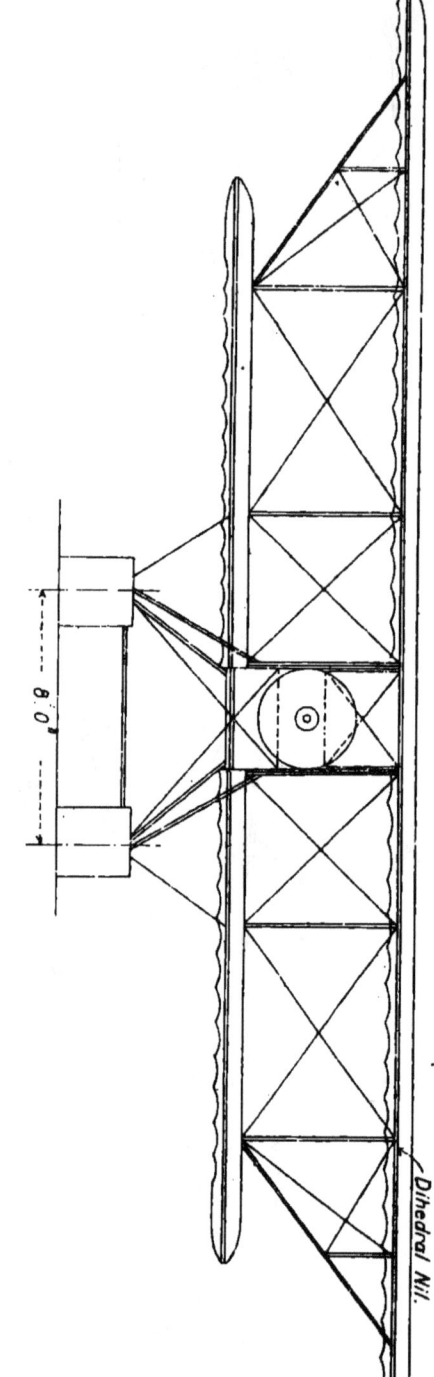

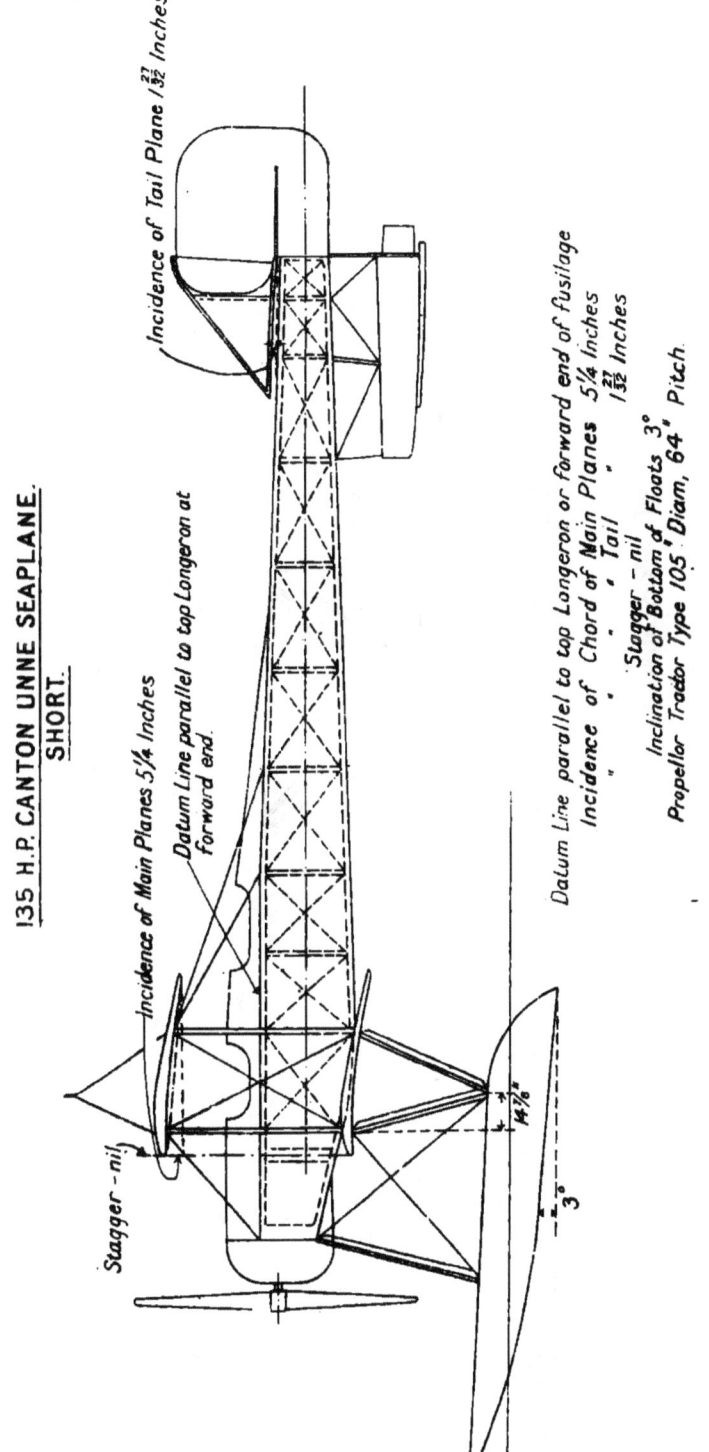

135 H.P. CANTON UNNE SEAPLANE.
SHORT.

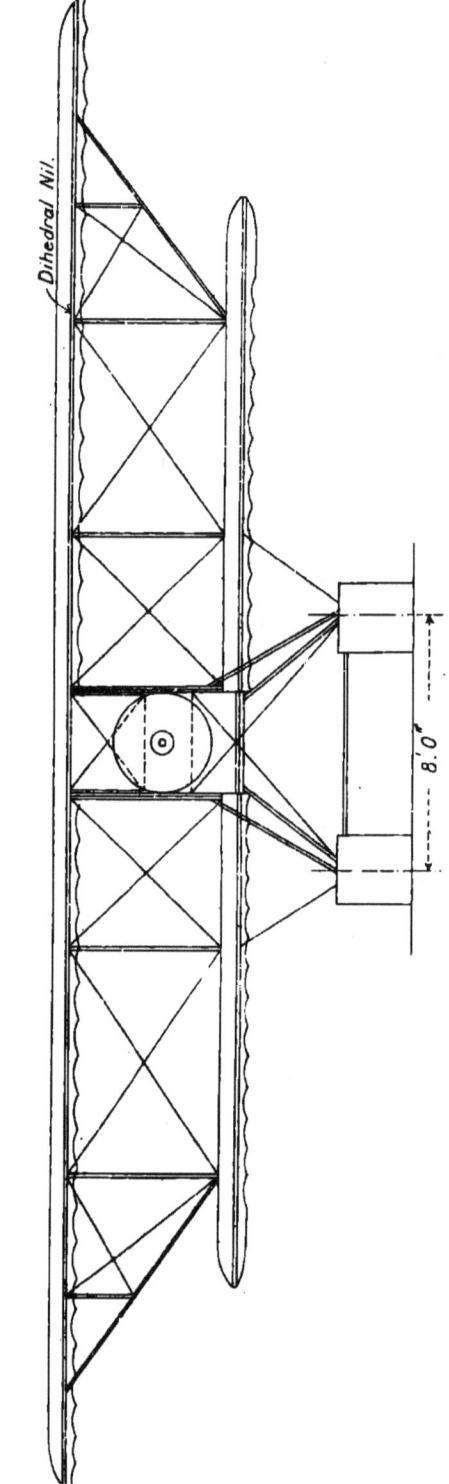

200 H.P. CANTON UNNE SEAPLANE.
SHORT.

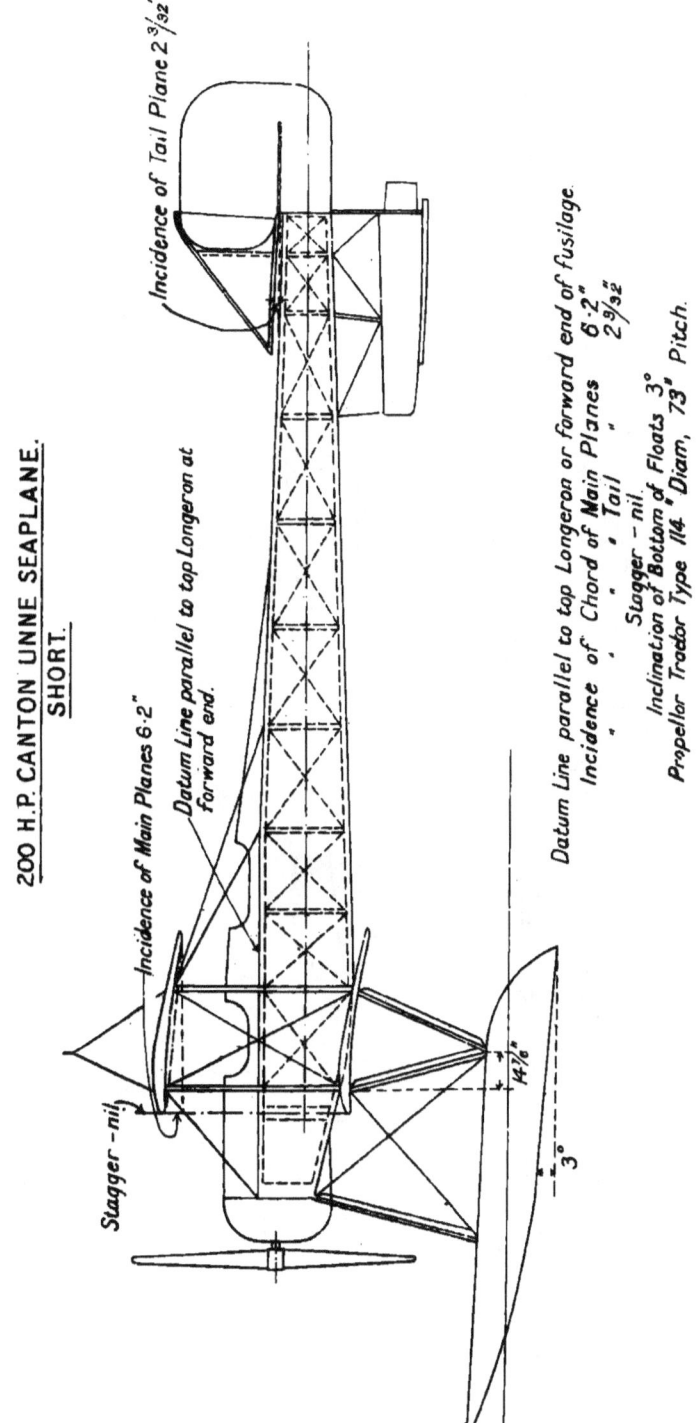

Incidence of Tail Plane 2 3/32"

Incidence of Main Planes 6·2"

Datum Line parallel to top Longeron at forward end.

Stagger – nil

Datum Line parallel to top Longeron or forward end of fusilage.
Incidence of Chord of Main Planes   6·2"
     "   "   "   " Tail   "   2 9/32"
Stagger – nil
Inclination of Bottom of Floats 3°
Propellor Tractor Type 114" Diam, 73" Pitch.

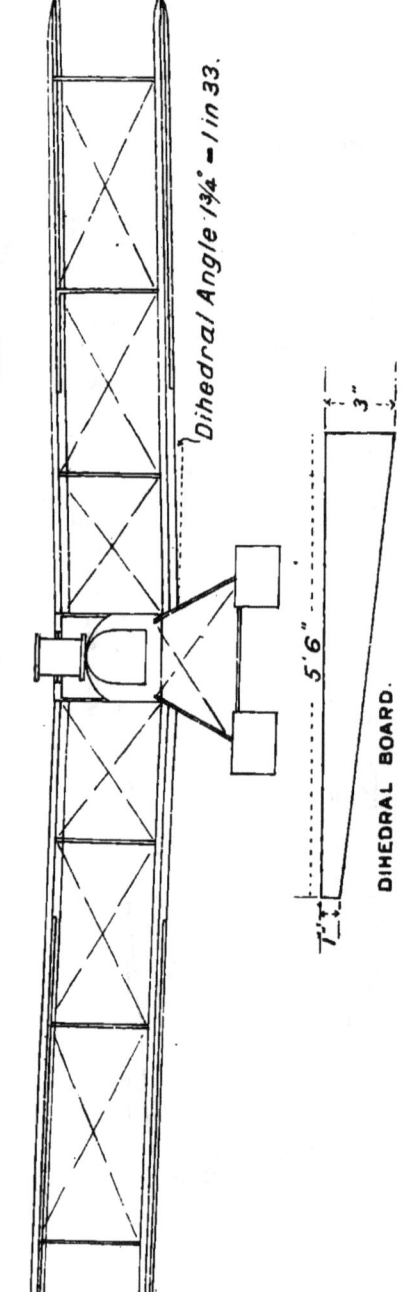

SHORT 225 H.P. SUNBEAM.
SEA PLANE.

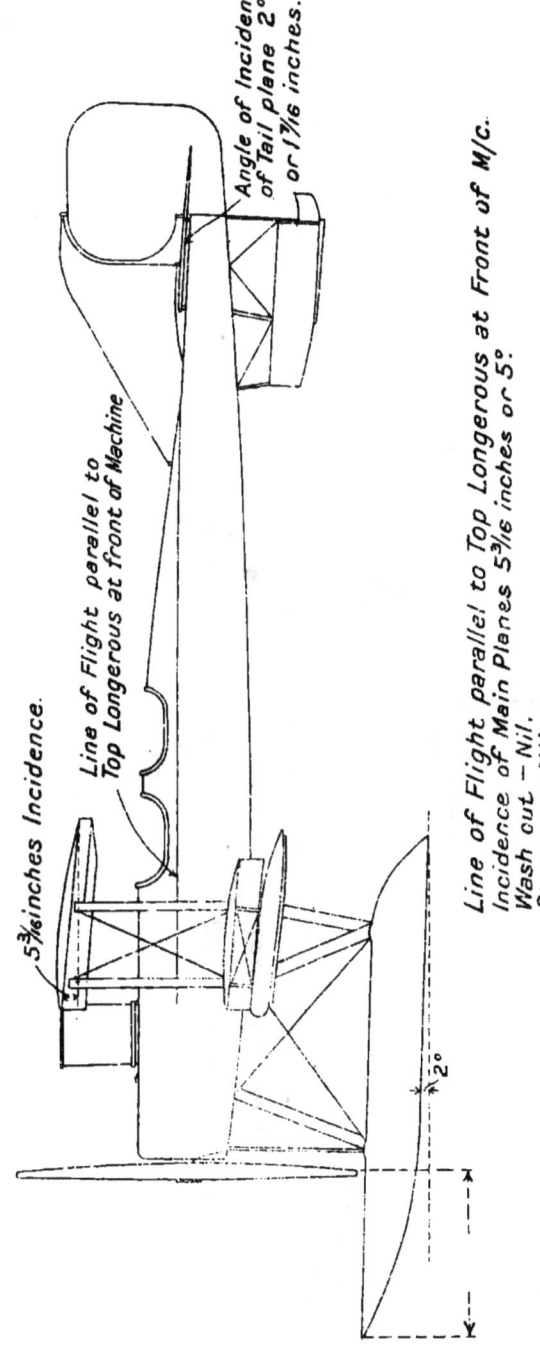

5 3/16 inches Incidence.

Line of Flight parallel to Top Longerous at front of Machine

Angle of Incidence of Tail plane 2° or 1 7/16 inches.

Line of Flight parallel to Top Longerous at Front of M/C.
Incidence of Main Planes 5 3/16 inches or 5°.
Wash out — Nil.
Stagger — Nil.
Incidence of Tail Planes 1 7/16 inches or 2°.
Throw back of Wings — Nil.
Set of Fin — Nil.
Angle of box of Floats 2°.
Propeller "Short" Type 10′ 9″ Diam. 81″ Mean Pitch.

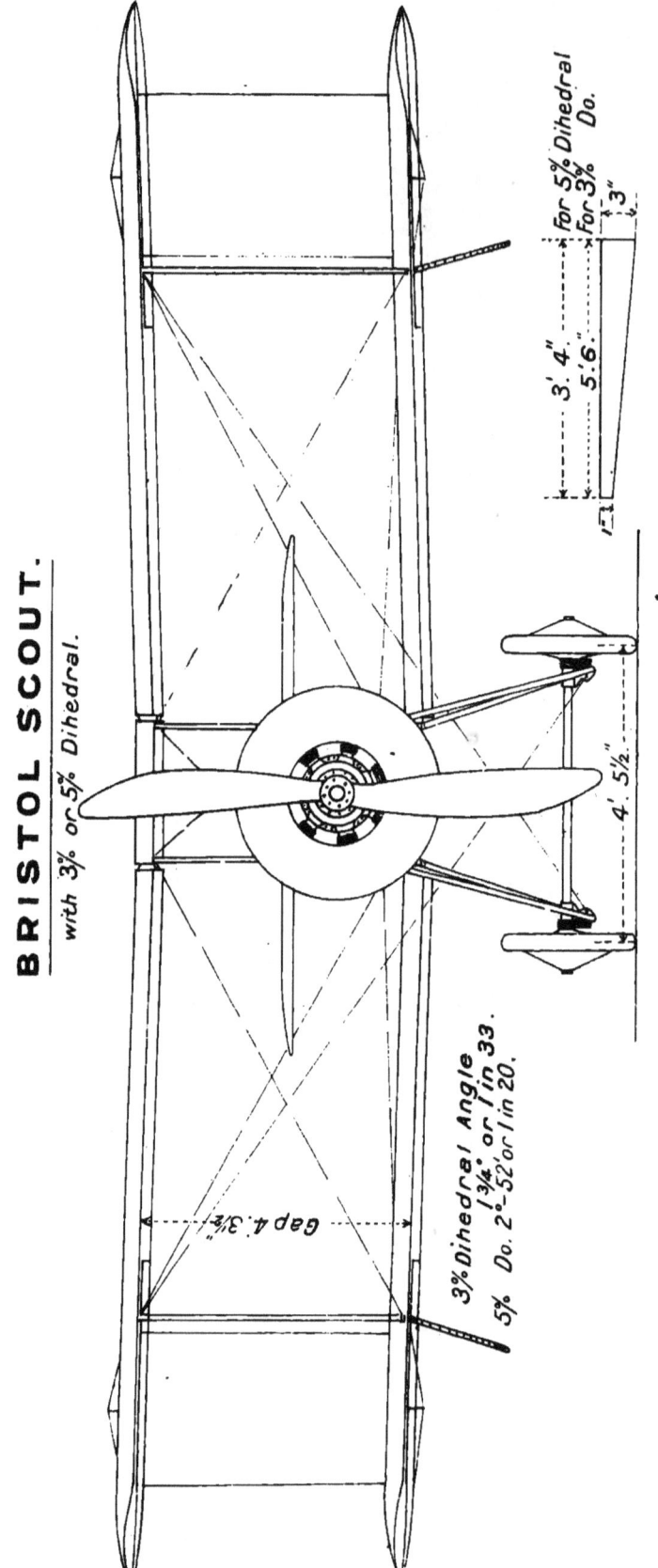

BRISTOL SCOUT.
ENGINE 80 H.P. GNOME.

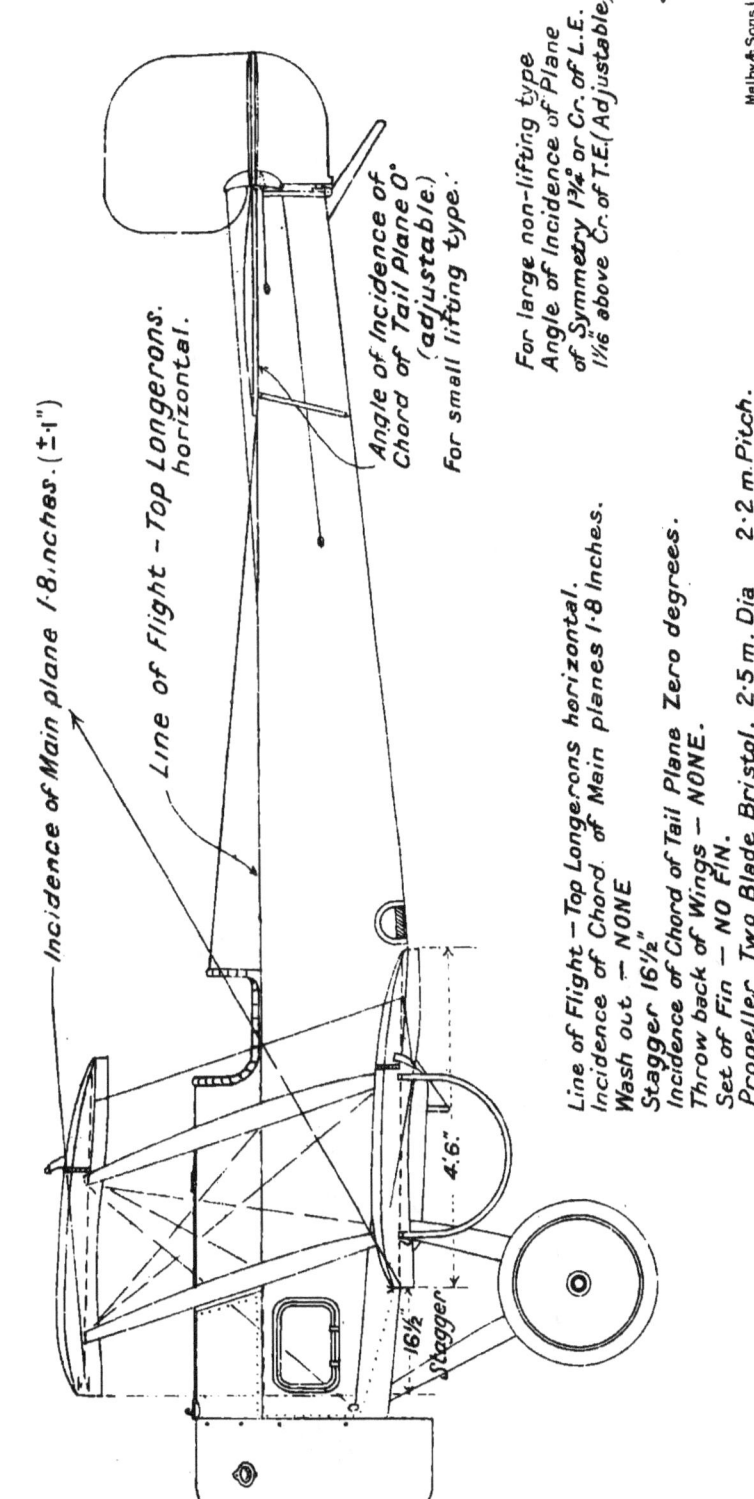

Incidence of Main plane 1·8 inches. (±1")
Line of Flight – Top Longerons horizontal.
Angle of Incidence of Chord of Tail Plane 0° (adjustable).
For small lifting type.
For large non-lifting type
Angle of Incidence of Plane of Symmetry 1¾° or Cr. of L.E. 1/16 above Cr. of T.E.(Adjustable).

Line of Flight – Top Longerons horizontal.
Incidence of Chord. of Main planes 1·8 inches.
Wash out – NONE
Stagger 16½"
Incidence of Chord of Tail Plane Zero degrees.
Throw back of Wings – NONE.
Set of Fin – NO FIN.
Propeller Two Blade Bristol. 2·5 m. Dia 2·2 m. Pitch.

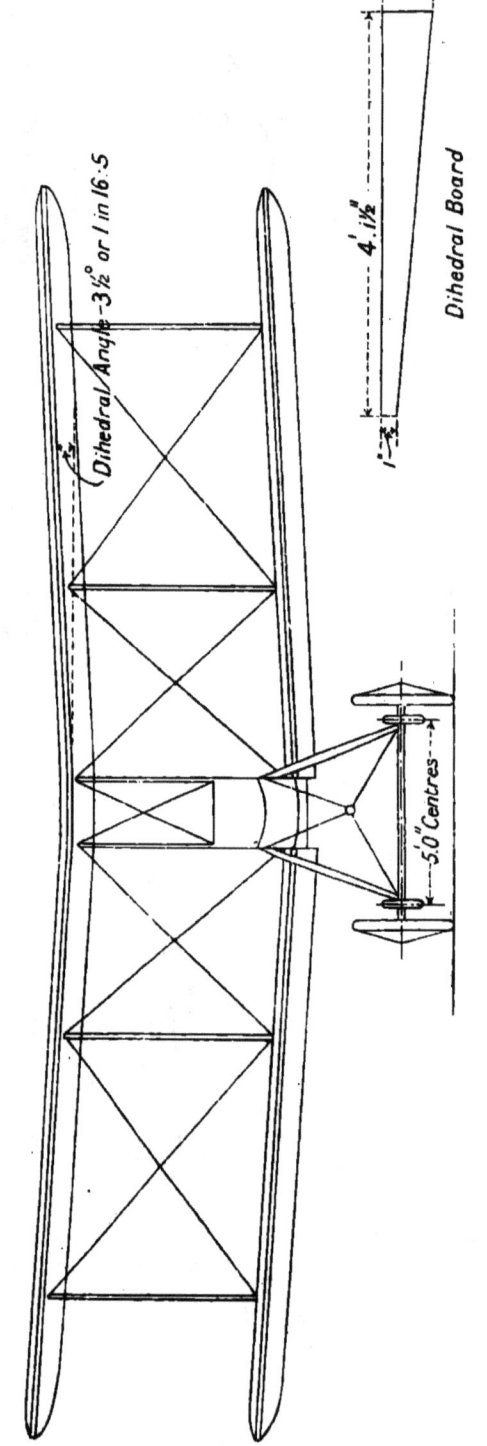

B.E.2C. MACHINE.

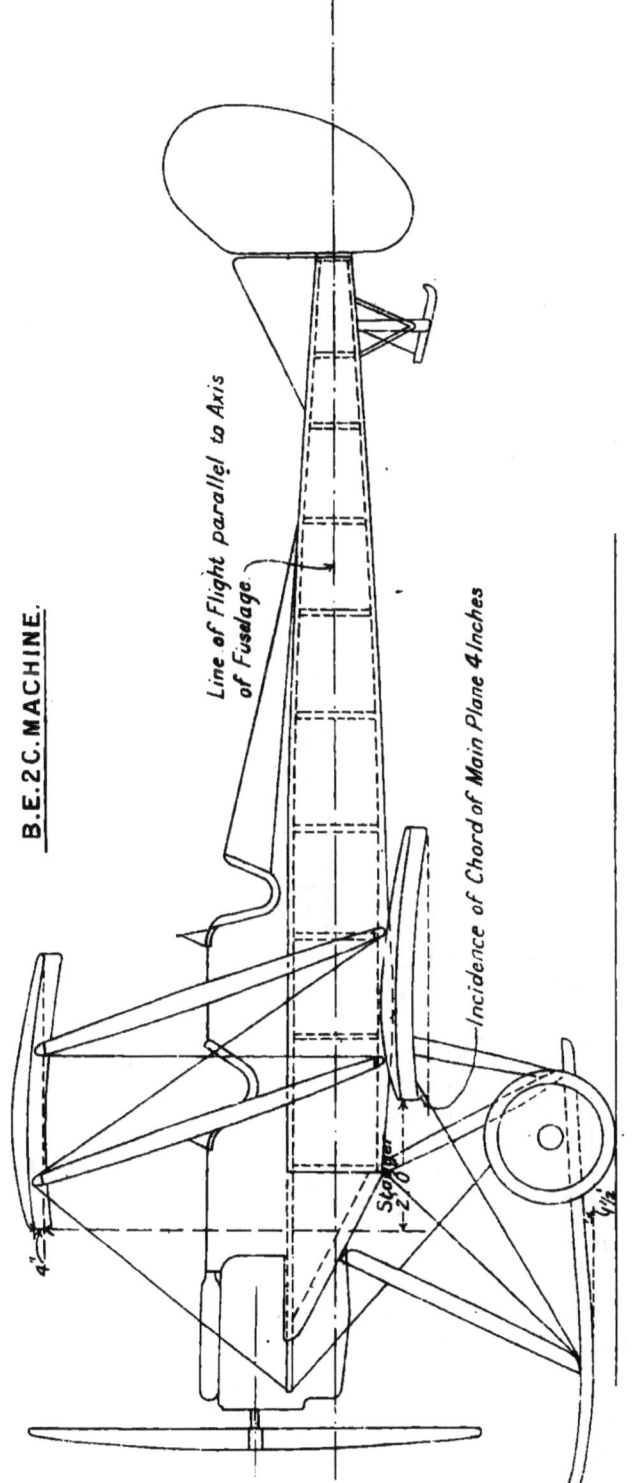

Line of Flight Parallel to Axis of Fuselage
Incidence of Chord of Main Plane 4"
Wash out – Nil.
Stagger 2' 0".
Incidence of Chord of Tail Plane Zero.
Throw back of Wings – Nil.
Set of Fin – Nil.
Angle of Skids 1½°.
Propeller fitted Special R.A.F. design.

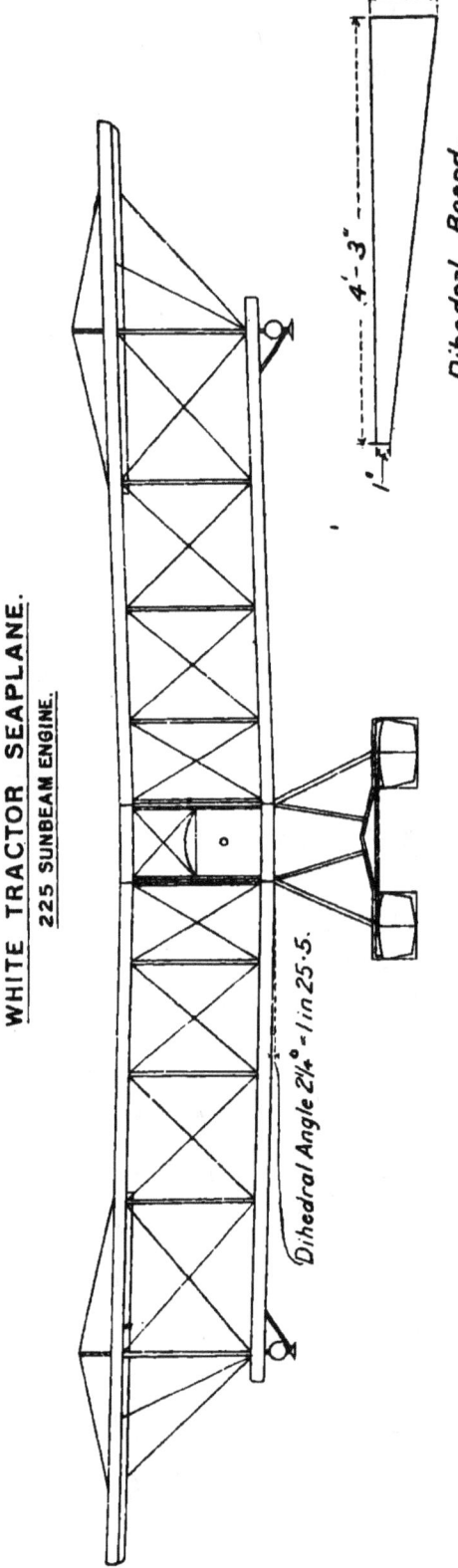

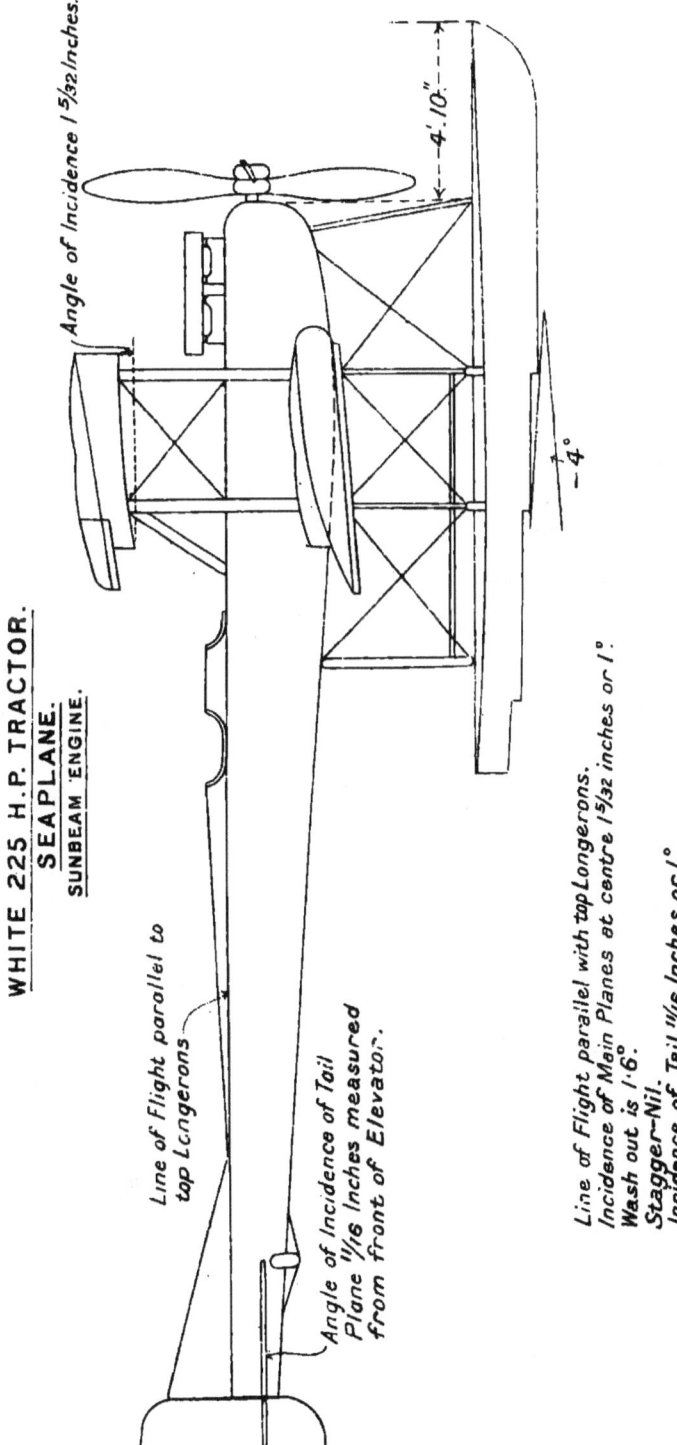

225 SUNBEAM
WHITE PUSHER SEAPLANE.

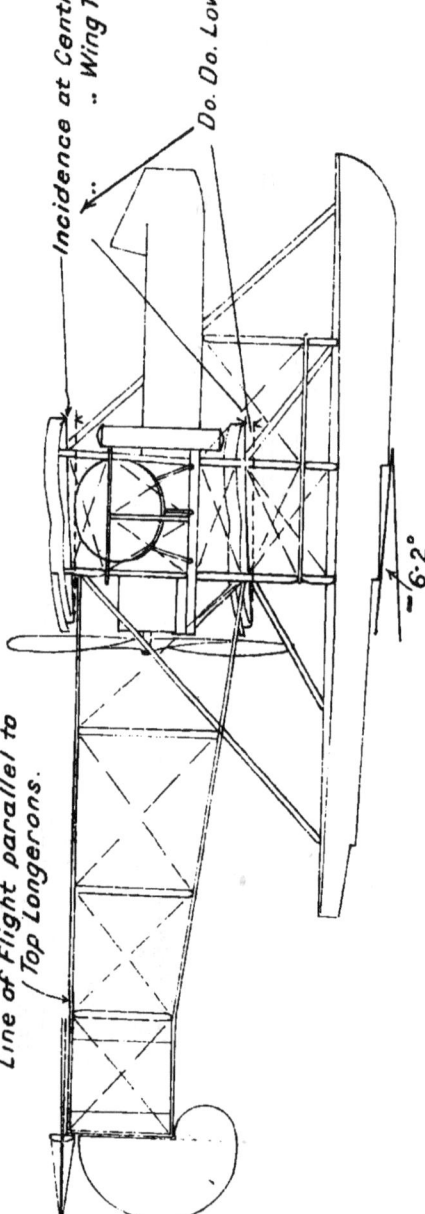

Line of Flight parallel to Top Longerons.

Incidence at Centre Top Plane 2 1/16 Inches or +1.5°
" " Wing Tips 2 1/16 Inches or 1.5°
Do. Do. Lower Plane 1 3/4 Inches or 1.5°

−6.2°

Line of Flight parallel to top Longerons.
Incidence at Centre Top Plane 2 1/16 Inches or 1.5°
" " Lower " 1 3/4 " " 1.5°
" " Wing Tips 1.5°
Wash out is 3°.
Stagger 5" on leading edge.
Angle of Tail leading edge 7/16 inches above trailing edge.
Dihedral Angle on Front Spar 1·04° or 1 in 55·2.
Throw back of Wings 1·25° or 1 in 46.
Set of Fin – Nil.
Front two steps of Floats 6·20°to line of Flight.
Propeller 4 Bladed Lang.

CAUDRON
G. .

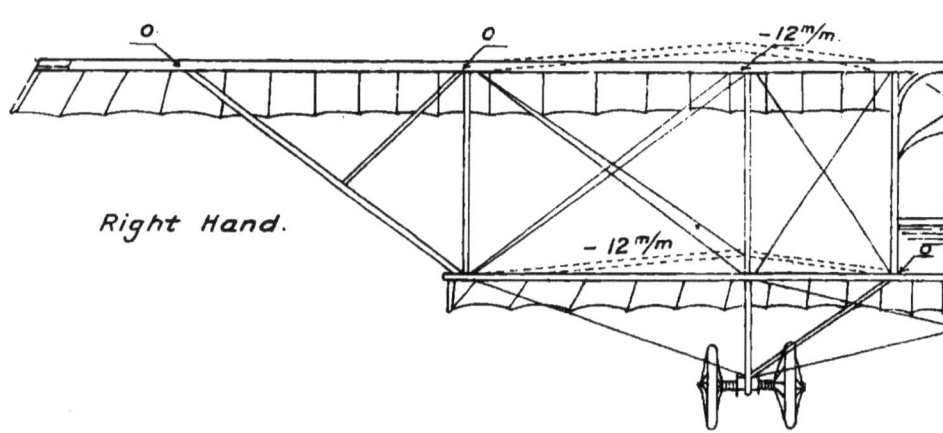

Right Hand.

The inclination of the

Datum Line. shown in sketch.
Incidence of Chord of Lower Main Plane 8⅛ Inches or 9½°.
......,, ... ,, ... ,, ...,, ..Top ...... , ... ,, ...12 ....,, ...,. 11½°.
Wash out — Nil.
Stagger — Nil.
Incidence of Chord of Tail Plane 4¼" Inches or 4½°
Throw back of Wings — Nil.
Dihedral — Nil.
Set of Fin — Parallel to longitudinal axis of Machine.

Stagger.

80 H.P. Gnome { Propeller fitted Grèmont 2·60 m. Diam.
1·45 m pitch at 1m from centre of boss.

100 H.P. Anzani { Grèmont . 2·50 m Diam.
1·90 m. pitch at 1m from
Centre of boss.

4658.

BIPLANE.
...YPE.

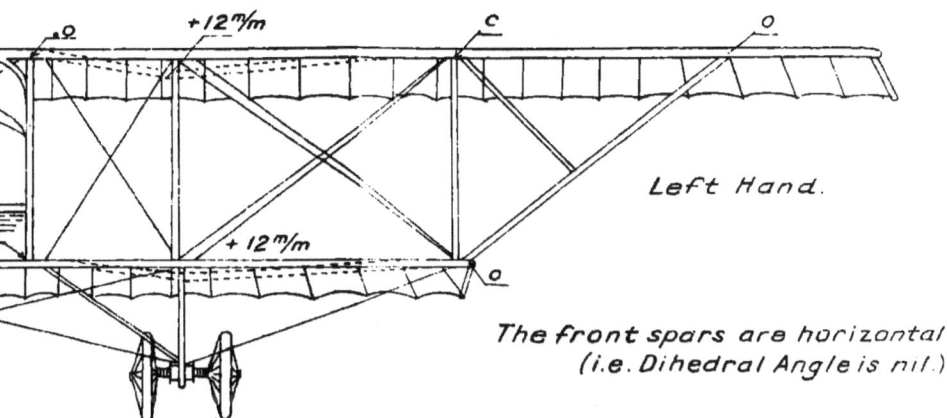

Left Hand.

The front spars are horizontal
(i.e. Dihedral Angle is nil.)

...ear spars are exaggerated.

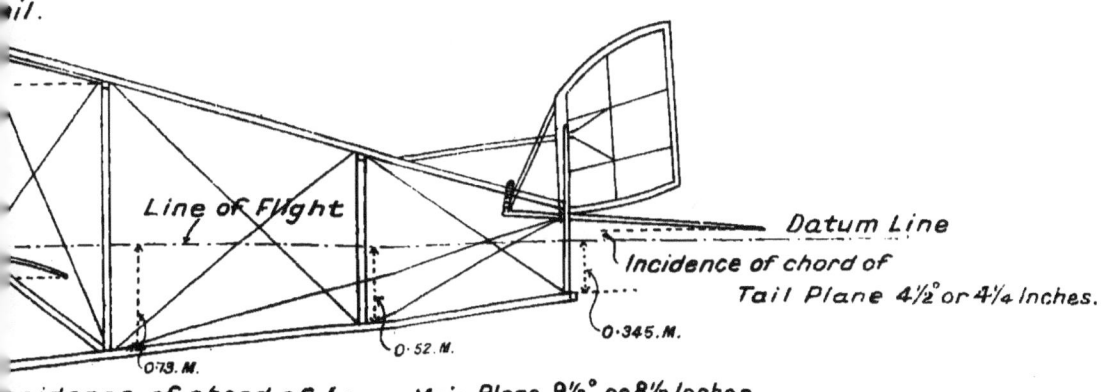

Line of Flight

Datum Line
Incidence of chord of
Tail Plane 4½° or 4¼ Inches.

0·345.M.
0·52.M.
0·73.M.

Incidence of chord of Lower Main Plane 9½° or 8⅛ Inches.
--- ,, ------ ,, ---- ,, --- ,, --- Top --- ,, ---- ,, --- 11½° or 12 Inches.

Malby & Sons.

www.ingramcontent.com/pod-product-compliance
Lightning Source LLC
Chambersburg PA
CBHW081508040426
42446CB00017B/3434